The Rule of Reason

a new approach to corporate litigation

MILTON R. WESSEL

The
Rule
of
Reason

a new approach to
corporate litigation

ADDISON-WESLEY PUBLISHING COMPANY

Reading, Massachusetts • Menlo Park, California
London • Amsterdam • Don Mills, Ontario • Sydney

ISBN 0-201-08583-6
ABCDEFGHIJ-DO-79876

To my good friends
Doug, Ken, and Mike,
who deserve the better
world I believe is coming

*"We have met the enemy
and he is us."*

Pogo

Foreword

As they enter the last quarter of the twentieth century, corporate management and corporate counsel are experiencing an accelerated pace of litigation as well as adversary proceedings at the administrative level.

This is the era of the class action, the intervenor, the consumer advocate, the public-interest lawyer. New laws—federal and state—pertaining to the environment, to health and safety, to civil rights, and to equal opportunity present new opportunities for private as well as governmental interests to seek from corporations remedies for wrongs both real and imagined. New statutes require interpretation. Often, interpretations unexpected by the proponents of the legislation will be advocated. Or, discrepancies and inconsistencies may creep into legislation and require resolution by the courts. Nor is it always the adversaries of the corporation who start the proceedings—or intervene in them. Sometimes a corporation must move as a plaintiff or an intervenor to obtain clarification of an obscure statute or to set aside a regulation or standard it believes to be unreasonable.

The field of product liability, certainly not a new one for corporate management and corporate counsel, has grown by geometric—if not astronomic—progressions in recent years. Very often there is an interrelation between product liability suits and new legislation dealing with such subjects as the environment or consumer protection. A public that perhaps was more inclined to accept things as they were a generation ago is now aroused and seeking redress. Manufacturers and sellers are held to increasingly high standards. Ad damnum clauses grow and grow—and juries are more generous in their awards.

All of this leads to the obvious conclusion that corporations must be more concerned than ever before with the conduct of their litigation. Not only must litigation be conducted in such a way as to protect the best interests of the corporation—in short, to win— but while the litigation is pending the corporation must show an honest and open face, one that will also enable it to win in that all-important "court of public opinion."

In *The Rule of Reason,* Milton R. Wessel has applied his own long and rich experience as a trial attorney for both government and private litigants to a penetrating examination of what is right and what is wrong with the way corporations conduct their litigation. He points out serious errors corporations frequently commit in their attempt to achieve successful litigation results. He pleads for a more open approach, contrasting the traditional "sporting" approach with his own concept of a procedural rule of reason. Not all will agree that the procedural rule of reason should be applied as completely as he advocates—but no one can deny that the concept is in the best traditions of the ethics of the legal profession. Hopefully, the low esteem in which big business is held by all too many members of the body politic might be at least partially overcome by following Mr. Wessel's theses. Moreover, as he points out, the rule of reason can be of great help to the corporation in presenting its case in a convincing and, hopefully, successful fashion.

Although Mr. Wessel has not intended this book as a manual on trial tactics, the corporation counsel will find it to be extremely useful in the management of his or her company's litigation. The book affords new insights into how to work with trial counsel and with management and scientific personnel in controverted proceedings, and that in itself makes it well worth reading—even if corporation counsel does not fully accept the procedural rule-of-reason approach.

Midland, Michigan WILLIAM A. GROENING, JR.
March 3, 1976 *Vice President and General Counsel*
 The Dow Chemical Company

Preface

This book is addressed to the managers of the legal function in the major American corporations, and business and legal educators. It is written with the hope that enlightened corporate enterprise will in its own self-interest take action that will have the incidental but sorely needed effect of improving the ethics of the legal profession and the quality of the trial bar.

Public dismay at the Watergate disclosures regarding the improper conduct of so many lawyers, and the burgeoning complaints regarding the inadequacy of trial attorneys, reflect the reduced esteem in which the profession is presently held. Lawyers are certainly very aware and very concerned. They are even less happy about it than the public at large, but there is not much they can do. American tradition is that the trial lawyer is an advocate, required to do his or her best for each client within the limits of defined law and ethics. Often the attorney has little alternative but to match the methods of the adversary, and the lowest grade of accepted conduct sometimes becomes the norm.

The law schools cannot do much more. Ethics courses tend to turn into debates over the fine line dividing propriety from impropriety. Trial law itself is very much of a practice specialty, demanding years of actual and live experience rather than tutorial or even "moot" court training.

It would be nice if one could repair the damage by preaching morality and professionalism. Certainly ethics must play its part, but Adam Smith has taught us well in this country that the human drive for acquisition and success is a compelling motivation. Quite probably it is the litigation incentive most calculated to produce the standard of conduct practiced. This book is accordingly designed to explain to corporate management, without preaching, why a new "rule of reason" approach to the resolution of disputes generally, not just "litigation" in the narrow sense, is essential to corporate success and even corporate survival in its present form, and why it must be adopted as a matter of sound business practice and economic well-being. The text seeks to persuade management to issue the appropriate instructions to their trial counsel, who will welcome the challenge and opportunity to practice their profession in a way the public will admire.

"Rule of reason" is not a new concept. Lawyers will recognize it as a long-standing, basic principle of substantive antitrust law. There it calls for adding up all the pluses and all the minuses regarding a form of conduct, and then basing the conclusion of validity or invalidity on whether the resulting sum is positive or negative. It is also the source of the traditional "reasonable man" approach of tort common law, where it sets the standard of conduct in accordance with what a theoretical "reasonable man" would do under the same circumstances. Its application to the resolution of dispute, the subject of this book, is as impossible to summarize briefly in this preface as it is to do justice here to its antitrust and tort applications. In those areas, volumes have been written on the subject. But if I were to select a single concept that would identify its heart, it would be the measurement of all proposed conduct by the test of how such actions would appear on "center stage"—as though whatever were said and done at the most secret or intimate moments were on nationwide television or the front page of the local press, subject to view and review by even the most antagonistic adversary. It is surprising how clear most applications of the rule become when subjected to this simple test.

Many persons and organizations are today struggling with the development of an acceptable standard of conduct to guide the modern corporation. The subject of this book is dispute resolution, not corporate conduct or morality generally. But it is worth noting at the outset that the far more difficult conceptual task of framing a sound code of general corporate conduct also becomes practical and even relatively simple when each proposed act is measured by the rule-of-reason test of asking how it would look and sound if televised nationally.

The stated objectives of the new rule-of-reason approach are litigation success and effective control of skyrocketing litigation costs. But surely no one will complain if along the way people begin to use words like "integrity," "morality," "honesty," "ethics," and "truth" to describe our system of justice and dispute resolution. Then will the legal profession be able proudly to assert its right to help lead society forward into the brave new world.

New York, New York   M.R.W.
March 1976

Contents

Exhibits

The New Litigation | Chapter **1**

Contrary to one popular misconception, the average so-called "consumer advocate," "environmental," or other "public interest" group is poorly funded and inadequately staffed. Even the government agencies advancing similar positions in the major socioscientific litigations frequently operate on a figurative shoestring by comparison with some of their giant multinational corporate targets.

Why then does the mere threat of a major claim or suit of this kind so often strike fear in the heart of business? Why do so many commercial decisions turn more on what "they" may do than on a well-reasoned analysis of the best course of action? Why do companies refrain from asserting rights they believe to be valid to avoid stirring up countersuits they consider invalid? Why are businesspersons concerned that punitive damages will be assessed against them for actions they are convinced were proper? Why is the response to a suit so commonly, "We can't win—we can only delay the inevitable," and the objective, a settlement or consent decree preserving only *some* of the rights or interests to which the company feels justly entitled?

The answer, of course, is that statistically these cases *are* frequently lost. The jury verdict, adverse but rendered without the imposition of punitive damages, and the antitrust decree, adverse but rendered without total corporate divestiture, must in this light be regarded as at least partial successes. What is behind these statistics?

Sometimes, of course, the business target of attack is just plain wrong and the corporation deserves to lose. Businesspersons are not all necessarily angels, anymore than any other group; the illegal, fraudulent, or sharp operator must be held responsible for misconduct and punished where appropriate. But this is a small part of the total of these kinds of litigation losses. And, as Watergate teaches, whatever the morality of the "consumer advocate," quite probably there are no more—perhaps less—miscreants in business than among their government adversaries.

Also, business losses are sometimes the result of an eighteenth-or nineteenth-century mentality—a failure to understand and appreciate the enormous changes that have been worked in our society, especially since World War II. There is more of this in our society than there should be. But this explanation is also inadequate. Modern American big business generally has had a poor public image. However, in contrast to public belief, a growing number of the officers and directors of our giant corporations is very much aware of and concerned with social problems. More frequently than is commonly understood, proper and sometimes even enlightened environmental, civil rights, and antitrust considerations are prominently included in corporate decisions. I believe this also is only a partial explanation for losses in important socioscientific cases.

I am convinced that a major explanation for the loss by industry of cases that should be won is inappropriate litigation procedures. Sometimes, in fact, those procedures appear almost designed to ensure loss. Unfortunately, the loser is not just industry, but society as a whole, because the issues are societal issues. Indeed, I use with reluctance the terms "public interest group," "environmentalist," "consumer advocate," and even "government" to describe industry's litigating adversaries in these cases, for these groups no more speak for the community as a whole than does industry. I once heard an industry witness define "environmentalist" as someone who tries to leave this world better off than when he came to it. In that sense, I hope we are all environmentalists, albeit each in terms of his or her own perceptions.

It is the purpose of this book to point out what is wrong with modern corporate litigation practice, and present and develop an alternative approach: the "rule of reason." I do this not for industry but for society, because, until industry's approach to the resolution of major socioscientific disputes is corrected and the litigating odds narrowed to what they should be, we will continue to have societal decisions that are less than optimum and therefore do all of us a disservice. We need something better.

Risk/Benefit Analysis

Litigation is of course a method for resolving disputes. The trouble with industry's present approach to litigation—in contrast to the approach of many of its adversaries—is that it fails to recognize that the key disputes have changed radically in recent years. That change in turn has changed the ground rules. In consequence, the old techniques not only don't work, but sometimes backfire with disastrous consequences.

Historical developments as fundamental as those through which we are now passing in litigation rarely have precise beginnings, ends, or other boundaries—at least not until viewed centuries later through the eyes of historians. But for current analysis it should be sufficient to take World War II as a turning point. Before that time, the majority of disputes involving industry were of the traditional variety: Was the contract properly executed or not? When and where was the injury sustained? Were the goods delivered in accordance with specifications? Sometimes these questions were difficult to decide, with many witnesses testifying each way. But somewhere, someplace, there *was* an answer—if one could go back in history with an accurate recording device, one could be certain that the answer was correct. Moreover, by and large the issues were of intimate concern only to the involved parties and their associates. Society was interested of course that "justice" be achieved in the determination of disputes, but most people really didn't care who owed what to whom or even (except when crime got out of hand) who was guilty of a wrong.

The civil rights, environmental, and consumer movements of the fifties and sixties, however, gave rise to a quite different type of dispute: that calling for the "risk/benefit" analysis. In this new type of case society as a whole, rather than any of the traditional litigants, must be considered the main party in interest. In addition, for the most part there simply is no absolute or categorical answer until after the dispute has been resolved, the decision announced, and a rule created to which all must adhere.

Safety is a typical risk/benefit issue of this kind. How safe is "safe"? Nothing is totally without risk, from driving a car (resulting in about 50,000 deaths annually in this country alone) to sleeping quietly in bed (fires are bound to occur and even buildings will collapse); from open heart surgery (high risk) to smallpox vaccination (extremely low but still measurable risk). The question always is: "Compared to what?" How much does one clean up a completely polluted lake? 50 percent, at minimal cost? 75 percent for $100,000? 95 percent, for $1 million? 99.9 percent for $50 million? To the last molecule, requiring the services and attention of every technical service in the community, calling for order of magnitude increases in the tax rate, and demanding the suspension of all present welfare and other social programs?

Consider, for example, the environmental litigation involving the marketing of a pesticide. The issue to be decided is whether the benefits anticipated from its use outweigh any related detriments. The evaluation of benefits involves subsidiary questions, such as how effective is the product in controlling the weed or insect? How important is the agricultural crop involved? What alternative pesticides are available and what are their disadvantages? How large a community is dependent on the crop for its farming livelihood? Etc., etc., almost ad infinitum.

The evaluation of risks involves similar subsidiary issues as to whether the product is or may be a carcinogen (a cancer-inducing agent), a mutagen (an agent causing genetic changes in subsequent generations), or a teratogen (an agent causing birth defects) and, if so, to what extent? Does it harm other desirable plants and, if so, can it be controlled effectively? Does its manufacture interfere with the production or enjoyment of some other commodity or value? Etc., etc., also ad infinitum.

The obvious difficulty of striking a balance is usually compounded by the uncertainties inherent in the evidence. The mutagenic impact of a chemical compound can be analyzed in a laboratory, on one or more species of test animals, for example, but extrapolating the results to other species or humans, and to larger populations, can only be done within restricted degrees of assurance. Thus, a test on 100 rats permits one witness to make predictions as to 1,000 or 1,000,000 rats, or as to mice, dogs, or humans, but only within necessarily limited statistical confidence levels. Therefore another witness, advocating an opposition view, can take precisely the same data and test results and quite validly point out that the admitted possibility of harm or danger should be evaluated differently. It is almost commonplace in socio-scientific litigations to hear numerous scientific experts, with equally outstanding credentials and reputations, testify one after the other, describe substantially the same data, and yet reach diametrically opposite conclusions.

Then, when one is all finished with what may be hundreds of witnesses, thousands of pages of testimony, and even millions of documents, one totes up all the pluses and all the minuses, somehow evaluates the inherent uncertainties, and finally makes a decision. If the risks outweigh the benefits, the product is banned or restricted; if the benefits outweigh the risks, the product can be marketed, although perhaps still with restrictions.

The immediate parties are interested, of course. The manufacturer learns whether and under what circumstances it may market the pesticide. The government and the environmental organization concerned, which by enabling legislation or charter are obligated to carry out a function, can measure the success or failure of their objectives. But the parties further down the line—the farmer, whose right to use the pesticide is being determined, and the consumer to whom the availability of the agricultural crop at a reasonable price can be of enormous importance—are interested most of all, even though they probably were unaware of the dispute until the decision was announced. The government agency involved and the public-interest organization may *claim* to be representing them, but they do not; the public's interests are as many and disparate as there are people and organizations, and no one speaks for them all. In a very real sense, these third parties are the vital parties in interest, although without representation.

Although it may not be so readily apparent, the other two most currently significant types of industry litigation, antitrust and civil rights cases, are very much the same in these respects. Except in a relatively few situations where decisions have been made and per se rules established, the issue is whether the conduct involved is "reasonable" considering *all* the circumstances. Often, the most esoteric economic and sociological evidence is brought to bear. Does a manufacturer's marketing practice constitute an unreasonable restraint on the trade of his distributor? Does a minority admission policy unreasonably discriminate against nonminority applicants?

Here again one adds up the myriad benefits and detriments in the face of "guess-estimated" evidence and makes a judgment as to which is the greater. In the *Smog* case, for example, the automobile companies considered their agreement to share antismog developments as a reasonable effort to abate pollution, in the public interest. The Justice Department viewed the identical conduct as unreasonable, and therefore anticompetitive and *against* public policy, because it eliminated an opportunity to gain competitive marketing advantage. These are the kinds of disputes with which this book deals. I term them "socioscientific" because of their general social significance and the scientific character of a major part of the evidence.

Several characteristics distinguish these new litigations from the old and call for different treatment. First and foremost, the absentee public is an important and often key party in interest. If our democratic society is to be responsive to the public's wishes, somehow the public must be enabled to cast the deciding ballot as to how its interest is to be served.

Second, and critical to the decision process, there are no absolute answers. Ultimately the decision must depend on how one values one set of concerns (e.g., energy), as against another (e.g., pollution). That decision will be affected by one's wealth, social status, upbringing, and perhaps heredity, and maybe even by what one had for breakfast or how a spouse acted the night before.

Third, and also to be considered in the approach to litigation, much of the evidence to be evaluated is of the most complicated scientific character, largely incomprehensible even to the intelligent layperson. If the lay public is to apply its own predilections and participate in the decision, it must in large part predicate its judgments upon conclusions as to whom to believe. Credibility—a misused but still vital word today—is crucial to success.

The "Sporting" or "Game" Approach to Litigation

Why do these differences call for a new industry approach to litigation? The answer requires an understanding of our common-law adversary system and its approach to the traditional cases.

One ultimate objective of any society must be to resolve its disputes in the most equitable way, all things considered. We call this "justice." Were it possible to have a perfect, omniscient arbiter, justice would inevitably be "right," given the rules society has laid down to govern itself. (There is no absolute way to test whether those rules are themselves "right." Slavery was once the rule in this country and the Nuremberg laws the rule in Germany; some consider our present property-right laws inequitable and antisocial.)

But, of course, we are all human. Judges are not perfect, and there is no way in which they can know all things. Most societies have learned that as a practical matter one can maximize the availability of relevant evidence to the trier of fact by relying on the self-interests of the aggrieved parties. To assist the parties, most justice systems also contemplate the use of advocates or attorneys, retained by each party to help in the presentation of evidence and argument of the facts and law. This is the "adversary" system—that is, each adversary, often aided by a trial-lawyer representative, marshals and presents its evidence and arguments.

Litigation systems are thus generally predicated on the notion that the self-interest of adversaries assures that what should be known is known. They do not anticipate that an adversary will go out and dig up antagonistic evidence or advance opposing arguments with the same fervor as those in support of a favored view.

In this sense, an "adversary" system of dispute resolution is common to most modern civilized societies. Systems differ, of course. In some, the court assumes a far more substantial role in the marshaling of evidence. In others, including the U.S. system, the attorney is far more of an advocate, even to the point of being encouraged to advance arguments and take positions with which he or she may not agree. Despite the inevitable failings of an adversary system, experience has taught that it is the best way of achieving justice among imperfect humans. I do not seek to change it.

But a special aspect of the adversary system has developed, particularly in the United States, termed euphemistically the "sporting" or "game" theory of litigation. This is litigation by "trick," with the lawyer achieving success for a client by procedural devices such as delay or obstruction, or *ad hominem* tactics designed to achieve success other than by dealing with the merits of the matter at issue. The malignment of adversary motivation is a typical example of the latter.

This approach to litigation—always questionable in my judgment—at least seems to work reasonably well in the traditional cases where all the parties are before the court, and where there is some absolute answer if only one can find it. The adversary system is based upon the ability of each of the parties to do its job; the tricks employed by one clever lawyer can be matched by those of an equally skilled adversary attorney. When one party is poor or otherwise unable to cope, the judge can step in to assist. And, unless there are strong community feelings, the jury will often help in the balance by its anticipated sympathy for the underdog. Furthermore, although some cases do go wrong, given enough witnesses and documents the chances are good that even the best lawyer cannot defeat a proper determination of who shot the gun or whether the contract was in fact executed on the date alleged. The statistical record of the "game" approach has been acceptable to society in the past.

It should not require extended argument to establish that this system is totally unsuited to the modern risk/benefit socioscientific litigation. The key party in interest—the public—is missing; there are no absolute answers; and the final decision must depend upon society's balancing of all the good against all the bad in light of how it wishes to live on this planet. The public may be willing to accept the "game" approach in strictly private litigations, where that method has to some extent demonstrated its value. However, the public cannot accept it where its own survival is at stake, and where the scientific issues are so complex and the ultimate judgment to be made so nebulous. In those cases the public's judgment must necessarily be based on its confidence in the decision process and the credibility of the participants.

Certainly the best known example of the "game" approach and how it can backfire is the General Motors-Ralph Nader dispute over the Corvair automobile. Although the environmental movement was already well underway at the time and would undoubtedly have burgeoned in any event, there is little doubt that this episode confirmed Nader as the movement's hero and major spokesperson.

The GM-Nader controversy is still raging, but the argument is no longer focused on what happened, but rather on the issue of responsibility. For present purposes that issue is irrelevant. Once GM had launched its admitted investigation of Nader's background, the "sporting" approach to litigation made it almost inevitable that someone somewhere down the line would begin the inquiry into sexual affairs, homosexuality, and anti-Semitism. That is the way the process works; to avoid it, GM would have had to take affirmative steps to insure that a different approach was employed—the "rule of reason" approach suggested here.

Nader was the author of *Unsafe at Any Speed,* a book critical of the automotive industry and particularly of the General Motors compact car, the Corvair. As of the month of the book's publication, November 1965, GM was a defendant in over 100 lawsuits involving potentially about $40 million in damage claims relating to the design of Corvair cars of the 1960 through 1963 model years. GM suspected that Nader, an attorney, was somehow involved in these cases. If its suspicions were confirmed, the investigation might disclose legal or ethical violations by Nader, involving trade libel of GM and the Corvair, champerty (encouraging litigation), or improper publicity, and possibly also provide useful evidence for cross-examination of Nader should he turn up as an alleged expert witness at any of the trials. Accordingly, GM retained a Washington law firm, which in turn retained a New York investigative agency to conduct the check.

All of the above is taken from the official statements of General Motors and its president, James M. Roche, to a Senate investigating committee. What happened next was certainly not specifically intended in the sense of anticipating the details of what was to take place. As Mr. Roche testified:

> Let me make clear at the outset that I deplore the kind of harassment to which Mr. Nader has apparently been subjected. I am just as shocked and outraged by some of the incidents which Mr. Nader has reported as the members of this subcommittee. . . .

> I personally have no interest whatsoever in knowing Mr. Nader's political beliefs, his religious beliefs and attitudes, his credit rating or his personal habits regarding sex, alcohol, or any other subject. Nor for the record was any derogatory information of any kind along any of these lines turned up in this investigation. . . .

> We in General Motors certainly would not want any private citizen to think for one moment that he was not free to criticize our corporation or products, before this subcommittee

or anyone else, without fear of retaliation or harassment of any kind." *

But irrespective of specific purpose and intent, surveillances *were* conducted, Nader *was* followed, and questions of the most intimate personal character were asked of friends, associates, and others regarding sex life, religious attitudes, and the like. When it all came out, the consequences to General Motors were immediate and disastrous. Its corporate credibility and image, which it tried so hard to enhance, plummeted. Its Corvair, which by 1967 had by far the lowest single-car crash rate of the leading compacts (0.16 per million miles, versus 0.24 for the Valiant, 0.55 for the Falcon, and 0.56 for the Volkswagen), had so fallen in public esteem that production had to be halted in 1969. The public understandably interpreted the effort to "get" something on Ralph Nader by investigating his sex life and his religious beliefs as an admission that GM knew it couldn't win on the merits of its case for Corvair safety—the only issue in the litigations insofar as the public was concerned. The *ad hominem* approach had thus backfired.

The fact, of course, is that GM's specific purpose and intent as to the kind of investigation to be conducted made no difference. The public held GM responsible because it had initiated the forces which led inevitably to the harassment and misconduct. As the GM witnesses testified, surveillances and intimate questioning are standard in background checks of the kind requested. It is thus the current litigation process, of which such background checks are a part, which is at fault; one who starts that process in motion does so at his peril.

Another more recent and even more revealing example of the "game" process at work occurred during the 1973 settlement of

---

* U.S. Congress, Senate, Subcommittee on Executive Reorganization, Special Hearing, 22 March 1966, Appendix, pp. 218–219.

the antitrust litigation between Control Data Corporation and IBM. Again, the facts themselves are not in significant controversy.

The Control Data–IBM antitrust litigation was one of a number of important antitrust cases in which IBM was defendant, including cases brought by the Department of Justice and Telex Corporation. The issues involved in all the suits were extremely complex, and the number of documents and witnesses almost staggering. Control Data had developed a computer method making possible ready access to some 75,000 documents, selected for analysis out of some 200,000 documents, in turn selected from some 40 million documents which had been inspected during pretrial discovery. Finally, the parties agreed to settle. As a part of the accord, they also agreed that this computerized access method would be destroyed. The destruction was carried out on a rushed and clandestine basis over a weekend, before informing the courts in which the actions were pending, the other parties, or the public.

When the destruction was finally disclosed, the Justice Department and Telex protested loudly and bitterly, charging that their reliance on continued access to the Control Data assistance had been frustrated and that their separate cases had been delayed and prejudiced. The New York Federal court, in which the government suit was pending, ruled that the destruction was in violation of a specific earlier court order requiring the preservation of such materials.

The important point insofar as present litigation procedures are concerned, however, is that not even the Justice Department or Telex seriously contended that the destruction was unethical or otherwise improper apart from any specific outstanding pretrial orders. Yet an extremely valuable piece of property had been destroyed, for no reason except to prevent others from gaining quick and inexpensive access to the facts. The most that was said about the obvious societal loss resulting from such destruction was the brief dictum comment in a memorandum opinion of the

Minnesota federal court, to which Telex had appealed for relief, denying Telex's motion, but stating:

> Though the court is not called upon in this proceeding to pass upon nor to opine concerning compliance with the Code of Ethics by Control Data and IBM counsel and their clients, the court does not mean in any sense or for a minute to countenance what has transpired here; nor in all likelihood would the court have permitted such had Telex counsel anticipated the possibility and brought the matter to the court's attention after it knew of the possibility of settlement." *

IBM had anticipated that someone might suggest ethical impropriety. Its lead counsel submitted an affidavit asserting his belief that the conduct was not prohibited by any principle of law or ethics applicable to the conduct of attorneys. His affidavit attached in turn the affidavits of a dozen leaders of the bar from all over the United States, including former federal judges and presidents of leading bar associations. Each affirmed not only the ethics of destruction as a general practice, but the propriety of such destruction even where the government and other parties had been using the destroyed materials and were obstructed by their destruction. The specific questions, and the answers given by all (although sometimes in slightly different language) are as follows:

Disposition of Work Product in Settlement. Is it ethical in settling a long, complex, and hard-fought lawsuit, between vigorous competitors, involving multimillion-dollar claims and counterclaims, and where plaintiff had sought to encourage similar litigation against defendant, for the attorneys for the parties to agree as a term of settlement that attorney's work product should be disposed of, where at the same time care has been taken to assure that the original underlying eviden-

---

* Control Data Corp. v. IBM, 3–68 Civ. 312 (D. Minn., February 9, 1973).

tiary materials discovered (the 200,000 documents) will be preserved?

Answer: Yes.

Interest of Other Parties in Work Product. Would your answer to question number 2 above change if you assumed that the Department of Justice (or the attorneys for other plaintiffs) had cases pending against the defendant which made related claims, and had been voluntarily furnished by plaintiff's attorneys prior to the settlement, intermittently over a period of many months, with parts of plaintiff's attorneys' work product, and might well have benefited, in the sense of avoiding the necessity of doing some of their own trial preparation work, from the further furnishing of such attorneys' work product?

Answer: No.

The New York federal court, in a footnote to its opinion characterizing IBM's violation of its document preservation order as involving "unseemly behavior," acknowledged the validity of these views. It said:

Defendant has submitted affidavits from many distinguished lawyers which affirm the ethical propriety of destroying work product prepared during the course of litigation at the time of settlement of the suit. The court does not question these prominent lawyers, but merely notes that the statements which were solicited from them are not in the context of a pretrial document preservation order, such as that which is present here.*

And of course IBM and the court are right. It is not uncommon practice for the parties to a settlement to agree to destroy materials, with the objective of impeding similar claims by others.

---

* United States v. IBM, 69 Civ. 200 (S.D. N.Y. March 10, 1973).

But despite its apparent ethical propriety, the public understandably interprets such conduct as evidencing an intent to hide something damaging, and to obstruct the efforts of third parties to assert their claims. It views such action as totally inconsistent with a corporate claim that its conduct is proper, that it has nothing to fear from the facts, that it wants its day in court, and that when all the facts are known its actions will be found to have been proper and in the public interest.

And, as with General Motors, this public condemnation is precisely what happened to IBM. The destruction quickly became major news in the general as well as the commercial and trade press. The damage to IBM's reputation and credibility, which it also works so hard to develop, was tremendous and apparent, albeit within a far more limited group than as to GM. Although in this case I know of no public statements similar to Mr. Roche's (perhaps because IBM was subject to a court order limiting its freedom to speak out in some respects), it is fair to assume that the IBM officers and directors were equally surprised and concerned. Once again, few, if any, probably had advance specific knowledge that the destruction would take place. But undoubtedly this settlement *was* authorized by IBM, and from there on it was the process—the "game" approach to litigation—that did the trick. As a *Newsweek* article submitted by IBM to the court stated: "IBM also argued that the destruction of lawyers' "work product," such as the disputed index, is both *ethical and routine* after a case is concluded, a claim with which government lawyers agree." *

A party who pushes a flowerpot off a windowsill cannot escape blame when it hits a passerby below. Specific intent makes no difference. A party who authorizes settlement cannot escape being held socially responsible for the "ethical and routine" conduct that follows as an inevitable concomitant of the "game" approach to litigation. The only alternative is to change the approach.

---

* *Newsweek*, February 12, 1973, p. 3.

Opposition Tactics

Industry's opponents have learned what industry has not—that the "sporting" theory of litigation is industry's soft and weak underbelly. They know that the public will ultimately make the decisions in major socioscientific areas, and that irrespective of ethical propriety and accepted litigation practice, the public generally will interpret obstruction, delay, attacks on motivation, character assassination, and the *ad hominem* approach as indicating that the corporation must conceal something to win its case. Suppression of evidence in itself has always been powerful evidence of guilt, apart from whatever it was that was suppressed; flight from the scene of a crime can be a criminal defendant's most damaging admission.

Trial lawyers are not prolific authors and rarely give away their own trade secrets. But one with strong environmental leanings, Irving Like of the New York bar, has written a most revealing article* emphasizing "education of the public and consequent public support" as the objective of environmentalist litigation, with one key trial tactic being to cast the opposition in the role of obstructing the public's right to know the facts. Consider the following quotations:

As to the objective of securing public support:

> In an environmental case, such as one concerning the hazard of nuclear pollution, the public interest is involved and litigation as usual, with the standard scenario of an agency hearing, will not suffice. The administrative arena must be used as an educational forum to alert the public to the project's adverse effect on environmental quality.

> Since the hearing is part of a larger script staged to win

---

* "Multi-Media Confrontation—The Environmentalists' Strategy for a 'No-Win' Agency Proceeding," *Ecology Law Quarterly* 1, no. 495 (1971):495–517. Copyright © 1975 by the *Ecology Law Quarterly*, University of California, Berkeley. Reprinted by permission.

ultimate public support, each day of the agency hearing must contain, whenever possible, a dramatic and suspenseful event. . . . The intervenor must plan and time the disclosure of its strong points so that each day's coverage has the making of an important news story. . . . For example, reporters often write their stories or edit their tapes late at night for the next morning's newspaper edition or radio news broadcast. They may sleep late and not appear in the hearing room until the late morning or early afternoon of the hearing. This presents counsel with the problem of timing and spacing his cross-examination and presentation of evidence to coincide with the presence of the media representations.

Even more revealing, as to litigation tactics:

The intervenor must develop a strategy of motions and objections which, . . . when disallowed, cast the agency or applicant in the role of obstructing the quest for truth.

Questions or evidence which may be ruled out by the tribunal . . . will be reported by the media.

It might be responded that such tactics are themselves the epitome of the "sporting" approach to litigation. And so they are. But the ethics involved have been sustained by a tribunal under attack on at least one occasion, and the comments themselves were originally presented at a course of study on environmental law sponsored jointly by the prestigious American Law Institute and American Bar Association. Like it or not, this is what must be anticipated and met.

Nor does use of the sporting approach by an opponent justify its use in response. As General Motors learned, the credibility of the opposition is *not* the issue; they have nothing to lose—no product to market, no plant to construct. They are on the attack, with the legal right to use every lawful and ethical weapon in their arsenal. Use of the sporting approach by both parties might lead the public to doubt the credibility of all, with a "pox on both your houses," but where industry has the burden of demonstrating the validity of a course of action, such a result means loss. The defense can be vigorous and effective, and not only by turning the other cheek; but the defense can *not* "fight fire with fire" and employ the same tactics.

Indeed, it is not uncommon for the "consumer" opposition to itself employ the sporting approach, hoping to provoke an industry adversary into ever more open and flagrant use of this same tactic. The objective is then to lower the boom and charge that such conduct demonstrates industry's fear of the facts. It is a taunting approach and extremely effective, especially among those to whom "turnabout is fair play" has become dogma in litigation. Turnabout may be fair enough play, but it can also produce disaster. The sporting approach is not only industry's soft and weak underbelly; it is being used by the opposition as an affirmative weapon to pierce that underbelly and destroy the beast.

The Rule of Reason

Present litigation tactics represent a medieval solution to modern problems. Clearly a new approach is called for, designed to meet the new problems of today's world. To be successful, such an approach must acknowledge the differences between the major socioscientific cases of today and the traditional cases of yesteryear. It must recognize that there are no absolute answers to the important questions, but only decisions reflecting personal attitudes and predilections applied after all the benefits and detriments of a given course of action have been weighed. It must appreciate that the ultimate decisions will be made by a lay arbiter and public necessarily incapable of fully understanding all the technical scientific evidence presented.

How are such decisions made? In precisely the same fashion that a layperson decides on open-heart surgery, even though he or she has no medical or surgical expertise and will in any event be unconscious while the procedure is underway—by trust and confidence. I cannot avoid using the misused word again—by "credibility." Industry credibility is the key to an adequate presentation by industry of its side of the major socioscientific matters at issue.

The importance of corporate credibility is certainly no revelation. It has been recognized privately and publicly for decades. Even the need to emphasize proper corporate *conduct* to achieve credibility, as distinguished from corporate "public relations" and "image" programs, has been appreciated by at least the more enlightened leaders of industry. As a result, the larger corporations spend enormous amounts of effort and money on programs designed to enhance their credibility.

What has generally *not* been understood, however, is the need to achieve that credibility in litigation procedure as well. Corporate executives will issue statements expressing unshakable confidence in the merits of a case, a desire to have all the facts presented to the tribunal, and a determination to bring the matter to an expeditious conclusion (these assertions are implicit in a vigorous corporate defense in any event)—all the while that their counsel are employing every weapon possible to defeat discovery and delay a hearing. Sometimes one wonders whether the two even hear or understand each other. Then, when queried about the explicit (or implicit) inconsistency, the executive will refuse to respond other than to say: "The matter is in the hands of our counsel, in whom we have complete confidence." And counsel will only respond: "I don't consider it proper to make public comments regarding litigations in which I am involved." Would a patient retain the allegedly successful, experienced, and reputable open-heart surgeon who in similar fashion refused to discuss qualifications or credentials—and then repeatedly tried to postpone surgery? Of course not!

To achieve the essential credibility a new approach to litigation, the "rule of reason," must be applied. "Rule of reason," a concept often used in substantive law but rarely if ever in procedural law, means many things in application, and it is one purpose of this book to explain the rule's application in different situations. For summary purposes here, the concept denotes total consistency between litigation procedure and corporate fact and purpose. One cannot pretend, directly or implicitly, to want all the facts on the table and then adopt procedures intended to obstruct discovery. One cannot purport to want a trial at the "earliest possible time" and then make dilatory applications with no objective except delay. Irrespective of overt statements or claims, such techniques are prohibited as inherently inconsistent with a genuine conviction in the merits of one's case. They refute corporate credibility.

The rule of reason demands complete consistency between public statements, public positions, and even the most intimate internal corporate discussions and actions. Even if ethics and morality were not a consideration, one can no longer rely on *anything* remaining secret or confidential in the giant corporate structure of today, including privileged conversations with one's own attorneys. Too many people are involved in too many different places over too long a period; too many new issues will develop to change the bounds of confidentiality; too many documents are written and too many copies made; too many disgruntled employees will leave and aid the opposition; too many well-intentioned people will regard their own concepts of society's welfare as superior to any traditional rule of business confidence or employee loyalty. What seems best now may turn out to be worst later. A person acting alone has difficulty preserving inconsistency from disclosure; there is no way of avoiding disclosure of such inconsistency in the face of these myriad potential leaks. Private conversations may certainly be more frank, open, and free than those in public, but the rule of reason demands that their substance be the same as if made on "center stage" or on the front page of a newspaper. Had the Nixon White House applied this principle, history might have been very different.

The rule of reason does *not* contemplate that the corporate litigant will throw open its doors for public inspection. Especially in these days of so much environmental and consumer extremism, one cannot turn over all one's files and make available all one's scientists and technicians in response to every charge. To do so would be to invite such interminable claims and suits as to deter the corporation from its main objective of carrying on a socially useful enterprise. The rule of reason is a part of the adversary system and permits full employment of the tools of that system, including its proper defenses to discovery and pleas based upon statutes of limitations or of frauds. It rejects only the "sporting" approach of the adversary system, an approach inconsistent with credibility and conviction.

Wholly apart from considerations of consistency, the rule of reason calls for maximum disclosure of facts and opinion, and trial and decision at the earliest possible time. Such conduct alone will convince the lay arbiter and public of corporate management's confidence in its position, especially crucial in complex scientific issues that the layperson cannot understand but nevertheless must decide. The heart surgeon cannot conceal or delay without explained justification and still expect to achieve credibility. Of course there may well be sound reasons for nondisclosure (such as to protect a valuable trade secret) or for delay (such as to complete essential research and testing), but these reasons will not prove embarrassing or inconsistent if disclosed.

Finally, the rule of reason seeks to persuade by emphasizing the affirmative benefits to be achieved, and by using every proper tool to maximize effective communication of technical and scientific matters to laypersons. In these two latter respects, it simply mandates sound litigation technique. Indeed, viewed overall, the rule-of-reason procedural approach is simply good litigation practice applied to modern problems. If adopted, however, it must be adhered to in routine litigations as well as in the major socioscientific cases for which it is designed. A party cannot pretend to integrity of purpose and procedure in some suits but not all. The public will not believe such selective morality.

The litigation rule of reason is an approach reflecting an attitude, not a specific set of requirements. It calls for different application in different circumstances, and cannot be reduced to a catechism. In summary of what is to be discussed in the pages that follow, the rule of reason generally demands that:

- Data will not be withheld because "negative" or "unhelpful."

- Concealment will not be practiced for concealment's sake.

- Delay will not be employed as a tactic to avoid an undesired result.

- Unfair "tricks" designed to mislead will not be employed to win a struggle.

- Borderline ethical disingenuity will not be practiced.

- Motivation of adversaries will not unnecessarily or lightly be impugned.

- An opponent's personal habits and characteristics will not be questioned unless relevant.

- Wherever possible, opportunity will be left for an opponent's orderly retreat and "exit with honor."

- Extremism may be countered forcefully and with emotionalism where justified, but will not be fought or matched with extremism.

- Dogmatism will be avoided.

- Complex concepts will be simplified as much as possible so as to achieve maximum communication and lay understanding.

- Effort will be made to identify and isolate subjective considerations involved in reaching a technical conclusion.

- Relevant data will be disclosed when ready for analysis and peer review—even to an extremist opposition and without legal obligation.

- Socially desirable professional disclosure will not be postponed for tactical advantage.

- Hypothesis, uncertainty, and inadequate knowledge will be stated affirmatively—not conceded only reluctantly or under pressure.

- Unjustified assumption and off-the-cuff comment will be avoided.

- Interest in an outcome, relationship to a proponent, and bias, prejudice, and proclivity of any kind will be disclosed voluntarily and as a matter of course.

- Research and investigation will be conducted appropriate to the problem involved. Although the precise extent of that effort will vary with the nature of the issues, it will be consistent with stated overall responsibility to solution of the problem.

- Integrity will always be given first priority.

A Scientific Rule of Reason

The preceding rule-of-reason discussion deals only with decision *procedure,* the lawyer's bailiwick. But of course the outcome of any socioscientific, public-interest dispute depends on the *substance* of the issues involved as well as on the legal procedure by which they are resolved. The importance of the substantive area, and urgency of the need for action there as well, justifies brief diversion to that topic.

Clearly the scientific substance of what is presented must in all respects be equally consistent with stated or implicit purpose and objective. Especially where technical matters are involved, there is need for a scientific rule of reason which will help the layperson choose between esoteric alternatives. There has been work in this area, but much remains to be done.

The procedural rule of reason requires that the many subjective considerations involved in reaching a technical conclusion be identified and isolated, and not passed off as expert conclusion. This is a most difficult assignment in itself, for scientists have as many problems with self-perception as laypersons (including lawyers). Even when this task is accomplished, the public still requires help in deciding how to select among the alternatives presented. Some public choices may always have to be of the "gut reaction" variety, but subjective alternatives can be ranked and quantified so as to be better understood by the public, *if* scientists will employ here the same effort and dedication they have successfully applied to so many of the "hard" science areas. For example:

1. *Benchmarks.* Broader general dissemination of "benchmarks" (points of reference), published in advance and not in the context of any specific dispute, would help the public to compare new risk situations with known and widely accepted risks. The layperson could then contrast the carcinogenicity or teratogenicity of an entirely new and unknown substance, for example, with some commonly consumed substance, like cigarettes, aspirin, or table salt.

2. *Standards.* Similar widespread, non–dispute-related publication of professionally accepted standards would also be helpful. It would give the public a way to measure the importance of early disclosure and peer review; to compare the qualifications of individuals and institutions; to identify good and bad methodology; and to recognize the significance of the number and kinds of experiments conducted, of long-use experience, of amounts of research and testing moneys spent, and of other objective efforts.

3. *Risk acceptability.* Many groups, such as automobile drivers, smokers, and steeplejacks, knowingly accept high risks. A widely publicized educational effort based on sound scientific research and data, might persuade the public to rely on objective tests that would rank this kind of risk acceptance for application to new situations. Precisely how this might be accomplished remains to be determined, but perhaps risks might be broken down and classified somewhat along the following lines:

Willingness to accept a higher risk	vs	Insistence on low risk
control (auto driver)	vs	no control (passenger)
voluntary (smoker)	vs	involuntary (audience)
private (mountain climber)	vs	public (consumer of public water supply)
ego impact (cosmetic)	vs	survival impact (carcinogenicity)

In a paper presented during a symposium at the 34th Annual Meeting of the Institute of Food Technologists, Dr. Richard L. Hall outlined a quite different kind of proposal which also might help laypersons decide technical issues. He suggested a hierarchy of confidence to guide the public as to whom to believe in the debates between scientists. If generally accepted, such a ranking of credibility could be most useful. He proposed:

1. Believe, most of all, the group rather than the individual.
2. Believe the broadly based group rather than the specialized group.
3. Believe the group containing members representing *professional* constituencies to whom they are responsible.
4. Believe the group that includes some obvious experience, rather than one wholly "outside."
5. Believe the group less dominated by obvious self-interest or bias of any kind—institutional, commercial, political, or aestheic—pro or anti.
6. Believe the continuing group rather than the temporary group.
7. Believe the article published in the best-known technical journals.

8. Believe sparingly, if at all, the shrill statement loaded with extreme adjectives and references to personal motives. Strong words usually mask weak arguments.

9. Believe next to the least the lay enthusiast, the zealot in his cause.

10. Believe least of all the scientist, even the Nobel Laureate, commenting outside his field. He is the most dangerous, for he will appear to the public to be qualified, but actually is not.*

Consideration of scientific issues is far beyond the scope of this book on legal procedure, and the above admittedly superficial discussion is intended only to identify a need and encourage an attack. Certainly, however, scientists and their professional associations can do much to improve socioscientific decision making and dispute resolution, if they will undertake the work necessary to develop a substantive rule of reason to accompany the new procedural approach. Scientists are as much involved and needed as attorneys in the resolution of these important societal issues.†

Corporate Responsibility

Thus far, the corporate executive or general counsel may feel comfortable in the thought that the responsibility—and therefore the blame—is solely the trial lawyer's. However this is most certainly *not* the case. Trial lawyers are advocates of their clients' positions, within the limits of law and ethics. They are retained to achieve the best possible result in the particular matter assigned. Obstruction or delay may well appear to be the best approach to the particular case at hand, even if it may have other adverse consequences elsewhere. How can the trial lawyer know? He or she is not privy to the totality of corporate policy and planning, nor would it ordinarily be practical that the trial lawyer should be.

---

* *Food Technology* 29, no. 1 (1975):48–53. Reprinted by permission.

† Recent developments suggest that there is at least reason to hope the National Academy of Sciences soon will be taking an important leadership role in this area, to begin with a public Forum in late 1976.

Some senior trial counsel, successful over the years in playing the "game" approach, may well be so wedded to it that they will change only with reluctance. Quite probably most, however, would welcome a client who says:

> "I want you to present my case in the best possible light, but I want you to play it completely straight. We're right, we've nothing to hide, we want the earliest possible trial. I'm going to announce this publicly, and I don't want you to do anything privately or publicly, internally or externally, which could by any stretch of the imagination be considered inconsistent with our public position."

Trial counsel might argue; they might cajole; they might wonder whether the client had lost all its marbles. But they would be delighted to be able to practice law in this most professional way.

The solution lies with industry; the decision to apply the rule of reason must come from top management. And because the approach is premised on an intimate relationship between the company's litigation posture and its general corporate activities, someone must be involved on behalf of the corporation who is fully privy to all relevant considerations. It is my conviction that the result will be an enormous saving in litigation expense for the company—many multiples of the executive time involved. Whatever the economics, however, the rule of reason won't work by just dropping a litigation in the lap of trial counsel with a general policy pronouncement. To avoid inconsistency throughout, one must know corporate policy and at least the important aspects of all other possibly relevant action, including much that is not involved directly in the litigation at all.

The remainder of this book deals with the application of the rule-of-reason approach to management of corporate litigations. It is addressed to corporate counsel and to corporate general executives and managers who are not necessarily lawyers. Its purpose is to convince the reader of the utility and economic effectiveness of the rule-of-reason approach, and to serve as an aid to management in applying it. Litigation strategy and tactics will be treated. Some non-trial attorneys may consider that suggestions designed to achieve a more effective presentation are inconsistent with the underlying rule-of-reason theme. There is no such inconsistency, for the most effective presentation is essential to proper implementation of the rule of reason. After all, the new procedure is designed to achieve success for the position being advocated.

Finally, despite what may be the appearance of the remaining chapters to some, this is *not* a "how to" book on litigation strategy and tactics. Trial law is every bit as much a specialty as tax or patent law. The ultimate litigation questions, such as how to examine and cross-examine a witness, are left to the expertise of the trial lawyer, in whose judgment trust must finally be reposed.

The Role of Corporate Counsel

Chapter **2**

The function of corporate counsel in administering litigations is simply enough stated: It is to achieve the best practical result at the lowest reasonable cost. Corporate counsel are usually overworked, however, as are most other lawyers, and one measure of the qualifications of outside trial counsel has been their ability to take the ball and run with it without much supervision. In consequence, this litigation function traditionally translates pretty much into the selection of trial counsel, plus relatively minimal reviews from time to time thereafter to see that things are proceeding satisfactorily.

Such management of the corporate litigtion function is unsound for many reasons, whatever the litigation procedure, but is especially disastrous when the rule-of-reason approach is adopted. Trial counsel are an important interface between corporation and public; frequently they are called on to respond in the heat of battle with little or no notice. Except in very limited and special situations, they cannot be educated in all the important general policy and nonlitigation fact considerations. Moreover, their interests and perceptions are very different from those of the corporate executive. They are experts in trial tactics, strategy, and practice; they are *not* experts in corporate management and policy.

It is the responsibility of corporate counsel to maintain a sufficiently intimate relationship with outside trial counsel to be able to participate in, and if necessary decide policy matters; to judge the ongoing activity of trial counsel in all its major details; and to take over those aspects of the litigation which can be handled more economically or efficiently within the corporation or by a third party. This of course means tight management, which some might consider somehow "unprofessional." But it can be done professionally and with discretion, and is essential to effective presentation of the corporation's position. With tight management controls so common to other aspects of corporate management, any contrary course in the face of skyrocketing legal costs must be viewed with question.

Obviously the degree of litigation management should be

geared to the case involved. A minor property-damage claim will not call for the same attention and participation as an antitrust case. But even in a minor property-damage case, corporate counsel must assume some degree of responsibility—at least to assure that pertinent documents are available and witnesses have been seen. As U.S. Chief Justice Burger and other commentators have said, the quality of our trial bar is much too uncertain to justify total reliance on proper preparation by trial counsel. And even were it not so, there will always be some level of error and incompetence to guard against. Corporate counsel should insist upon at least some reports in every suit, and not leave cases on a back burner until trial counsel decides to call.

Corporate counsel need not have trial experience to manage litigations, although of course it would be helpful. But he or she must know enough about litigation to handle policy decisions, judge the effectiveness of trial counsel, and administer those matters which are his or her primary responsibility. These latter subjects will be treated in subsequent chapters.

In this chapter I will suggest some reasons why corporate counsel's participation is required, particularly in certain critical areas. But first, some definitions. I use the term "corporate counsel" to describe the attorney given general responsibility for the corporation's legal affairs. He or she is to be distinguished from outside trial counsel, retained to handle one or more claims or cases, and special counsel, retained to advise on one or more non-litigated specific matters.

Corporate counsel's responsibility encompasses the entire range of corporate affairs. If something goes wrong legally, management is entitled to ask why, and corporate counsel should have an answer. Although corporate counsel cannot know everything, he or she should be of a reasonably suspicious nature and should develop sensible measures for seeing whether matters are proceeding properly—*before* major problems arise.

Special or trial counsel, in contrast, ordinarily deal only with matters assigned. If something goes wrong outside their representation, their perfectly proper response to the corporation is: "You didn't ask me." Typically, their opinions will begin with a statement, "You have asked our opinion with regard to the following facts. . . . " If they have made an inquiry regarding these facts, they will describe the nature of that inquiry. Unlike corporate counsel, they assume no other responsibility for the corporation's legal affairs.

In the larger corporations most commonly involved in the major socioscientific litigations, corporate counsel is usually an employee of the corporation, and the general (or chief) corporate counsel, an officer or director of the corporation or both. But he or she need not be, and in any event I have not used the term "house counsel," sometimes felt to connote a "kept" attorney.

I also use the term "litigation" to include all aspects of the dispute resolution process, from earliest beginnings as a significant issue on through the claim and hearing or trial and appellate stages. Because consistency is so much a part of the rule-of-reason approach, and because there is no way for a corporation to distinguish to the public what it says during precourt proceedings and thereafter, this inclusive definition is essential.

Law Firm Management

Law firms consider their management affairs most confidential, and are not notable complainers. Perhaps as a consequence, few corporation executives or their employee lawyers appreciate law firm management problems and concerns. Yet those problems are just as substantial as those incident to any business, and perhaps more so. They often result in such different perceptions regarding the course of action to be pursued as to mandate special attention by corporate counsel to areas such as fact preparation (Chapter 3), billing and attorney assignment (Chapter 4), and settlement (Chapter 5).

A word about perceptions: The Declaration of Independence statement "all men are created equal" has never meant the same thing to all men, black or white, or to all women. Anyone who has tried an automobile negligence case knows that ten witnesses, all trying honestly to tell the truth, will relate ten different stories. We believe what we sense, and what we sense is determined by innumerable factors—including what we want and need, what we like, what we dislike, our ambitions, everything. I hope no one will consider it unfair or critical of me to suggest that a law firm earning a million-dollar annual litigation fee (representing an important part of its gross volume) may look at a settlement proposal ending that litigation somewhat differently than the client paying that fee. Conceivably the firm may even lean over backwards to *accept* the settlement, in an effort to avoid being unduly influenced by what it recognizes are its own financial interests independent of and perhaps adverse to the client's. But whatever the action taken, those interests are necessarily different and the resulting perceptions must be judged in that light.

Law firms are professional organizations, but they are also very much in business to earn a profit. Like all other businesses, they have peaks and valleys of work, good and less-good attorneys, training programs, management controls, issues as to how to charge for services, and problems as to how to compensate personnel for work done. If one is staffed to handle the peak anticipated workload (few are), what happens to surplus attorneys during the lulls? If staffed to average, who suffers when a peak or emergency comes along? Who gets the "less-good" or slower attorney? What happens when a rotation training program calls for the shift of an attorney working on and intimately informed about a lengthy litigation? Where there is more than one hourly rate for an attorney (as is common), who gets the lower rate and who the higher? When one must travel to a city to interview a witness *and* attend a bar convention, who pays the travel expenses? Who gets charged for the travel time? What is the approach of an ambitious young attorney to the substantial discretion involved in reporting time charges, when he or she has just been told by a senior partner that work hours reported are far below average?

What is the reaction when the attorney has been told that he or she is slow, and turns out much less work than law-firm peers during the same time? Does the partner who is receiving "credit" for having brought in a valuable client and is anxious not to lose the client render billings differently than the "working" partner who gets "credit" based strictly on the work put in?

In another connection, law firms as well as their corporate clients have reputations to protect and enhance. Professionals whose careers are dependent upon reputation and recommendation are necessarily cautious in how they proceed. They know from bitter experience that even a long and untarnished career can be damaged or destroyed by a single misstep. This produces other concerns: Wholly apart from any technical conflict considerations, how does the firm view a tactic that could potentially antagonize a judge in a court in which it is practicing? How does it deal with a proposed argument that may be inconsistent with a position being advocated for another client? Are there cases in which the firm's reputation calls for the submission of a detailed legal memorandum, even if on analysis the economics might not justify it for the client involved? Might a firm want to "win" a case assigned, even if another case elsewhere, handled by a competing firm, might be the better test vehicle?

In still a third and totally different connection, the client's and the firm's interests differ even in regard to the level at which the work is to be handled. The firm's interest is that the work be handled at the lowest reasonable professional level; the client's interest is (or should be) that it be handled at the highest. It is surprising how few clients appreciate this reality. They would prefer that work be done by a $40 per hour associate, just out of law school, or a $25 per hour paralegal assistant, not an attorney at all, rather than by a $125 per hour senior-level partner. They don't understand that senior attorneys, who have the benefit of years of experience, should operate with much greater efficiency, for they know precisely what they want and don't have to revise and rerevise to suit someone else's preferences. In addition, the senior attorney must know much of what the junior is doing anyway if he or she is to handle the matter effectively and also adequately administer the firm's training program. Clients generally don't realize how much time is wasted by the young attorney writing and correcting memorandum reports to the senior of everything that happens; how much money the firm earns on its junior people—the paralegal is the best economic development for the legal profession in years; and how much money could be saved and training accomplished by doing low-level work in-house. Often clients come to the trial law firm seeking special outside expertise, and then insist on the assignment of people less qualified than their own staffs!

To state all these questions is not to answer them; I hope to do that in the following chapters. But it should be sufficient to make clear that corporate counsel has a major responsibility to participate in the trial law firm's management of its operations, at least insofar as in determining what work should be done and when, what work should not be done, what assignments and reassignments of personnel should be made, and how billing should be handled. Where settlement is involved, corporate counsel should take an especially active role, personally participating in the negotiations where appropriate and sometimes even taking over completely (although usually still in consultation with trial counsel).

The above factors necessarily contribute to a difference in viewpoints between corporate counsel and law firms generally. But another unique set of factors applies especially to trial lawyers.

The economics of trial law are a thing unto themselves. Many of the trial attorney's cases are "one-shots" for clients he or she will never see again; long-term understandings and relationships have little chance to flourish. Families must be fed and children educated; many successful trial lawyers accept more cases than they can reasonably handle—to be sure that they'll continue to be busy if the current case is settled or adjourned. While actually on trial, the diligent trial lawyer must devote his or her total attention to a single matter, day and night, necessarily ignoring in large part everything else that is going on. Yet by far the largest part of his or her cases are settled on the courthouse steps, encouraging risks in underpreparation.

Some years ago I sat as a member of one of the court committees of a local bar association. The delays in that court from the date of filing a "note of issue" (the document which places the case on that court's calendar for trial) to trial were horrible, averaging more than five years. We continually protested to the elected chief judge, who kept responding that the problem was the fault of the lawyers, not the court. He claimed the lawyers repeatedly adjourned cases by stipulation, even after they filed notes of issue certifying that the cases were in all respects ready for trial. Finally he proved his point to us by inaugurating a new procedure, simply prohibiting adjournments (except for the most compelling of reasons) once a note of issue was filed. The five-year delay between filing of note of issue and trial vanished overnight when counsel appreciated that the game was over—when they indicated they were prepared by filing a note of issue they had better mean it. But the delay between date of filing the first pleading and time of trial stayed exactly the same; all that had been accomplished was to shift the delay period back, to precede the filing of the note of issue! The fault was indeed that of the trial lawyers, at least in large part.

It is an unfortunate fact that all too often litigations are ignored or forgotten until pressure from an adversary or a court— or a client—requires that something be done. Attorneys assigned to the case will be switched to handle urgent matters elsewhere, jeopardizing preparation; thereafter they will sometimes be transferred back when the emergency has passed, even though careful analysis might have shown that some of the effort is no longer strictly needed. Where the client doesn't demand attention, all too often no one seems to really give a damn.

Claims Administration

The modern corporation often processes thousands of "claims," i.e., issues perceived as likely to generate significant differences of view. There is no precise time when a claim matures into something requiring intimate legal participation. But even the administration of claims is an area in which corporate counsel must take the lead. Except in instances when the claims department of the corporate insurance carrier is involved, there is ordinarily no experienced adjuster supervising the matter. Yet quite commonly the case is made or lost at this stage. General corporate employees who are not attorneys are still very much in the picture, making statements and taking positions which are as much a part of the total record of corporate conduct as the transcribed record of the subsequent trial.

Consistency of corporate action has no beginning or end; a witness cannot explain away deviousness, or obstruction, or dilatory tactics by reference to the early time at which something took place. Trial practice teaches that evidence arising *ante litem motam* (before the dispute motivation arose) is entitled to greater credit than that which comes later.

In the large corporate structure, it is ordinarily impossible for corporate counsel to be involved personally in every difference or claim at its inception. But that need not prevent counsel from playing the part required by the rule-of-reason approach. It is his or her responsibility to see that the methods applied in resolving claims are the same as those employed in handling later aspects of the same controversy. General training programs can communicate the essentials of corporate policy in this regard, in the same fashion as they do other matters. The handling of major portions of litigation fact preparation in-house, to be discussed in Chapter 3, will gradually build an increasingly large cadre of internal paralegal personnel knowledgeable in the process. And the corporate claims department and field attorneys can intensify efforts to become involved in issues at ever earlier times.

Corporate Counsel's Management Function

The general counsel of a corporation is its chief attorney, but he or she is also very much a part of its general management. This latter aspect of the general counsel's function is too frequently overlooked.

Our major corporations are struggling today with the most difficult and complex of problems. At what point have research and testing gone far enough to justify marketing a new drug or chemical? Are there as yet unobserved but dangerous side effects from a given manufacturing process, or a mining or land-clearing policy? What will be the economic effects of a new licensing or franchising arrangement? Many executives ponder such issues day and night, seeking desperately to find the best solutions.

There is no clear answer to these kinds of questions, of course. But the law department can be of enormous help if it will only marshal its information and enter it into the management decision process. It is the place in the corporation where objections, differences of view, and claims are concentrated. Often warning signals can be perceived by the law department long before any problem has been observed by others, and always before litigation (in the courtroom sense) is in sight. If the law department will collect these items of evidence and classify them by product, manufacturing process, geographic area, and other relevant respects, it can serve as a kind of very early-warning center, alerting the rest of the company that corrective action may be indicated. In a very real and important sense, its empirical analysis will help develop the solutions to these otherwise almost impossible problems.

In our increasingly complex and regulated society, the role of corporate counsel is vital to the corporation's well-being and sometimes to its survival. The rule-of-reason approach renders it even more so.

Preliminary Preparation

Chapter **3**

The law regarding socioscientific litigations is new and developing rapidly, and of substantial interest and importance. The development of sound legislative approaches to socioscientific problems may be one of our most difficult assignments, but analysis of this area of the law in a litigation context is relatively simple. It represents only a small fraction of the effort involved in most of the really "big" cases. Presentation and argument of such law are also significant, of course, but ordinarily there is not a great deal one can do individually to affect the final decision on the legal issues. That will be determined by events and circumstances beyond one's effective control, including the actions of legislatures and general societal trends, and the decisions of other courts at the same level and on review. Instead, facts are the heart of the major socioscientific case.

Prompt, thorough investigation of the facts is the single most important part of corporate counsel's responsibility in these cases. Ordinarily it must be undertaken even before trial counsel has been retained, yet how it is handled may well predetermine the case from every aspect, including litigation tactics and strategy as well as trial and appellate presentation and cost. It is worth considering some of the reasons for this before turning to fact preparation techniques.

Consistency is essential to the corporation's credibility in socioscientific cases. The lay community cannot be expected to understand the esoteric science involved, and will react immediately and adversely to unjustifiable changes in the corporation's story. I believe the growing tendency of courts to impose punitive damages in so many of these cases is because of changes in the factual presentation *after* the dispute arises, not because of any improper underlying conduct. The judge or jury naturally becomes convinced that corporate or attorney disingenuity or fabrication is involved. Lay people cannot understand how a corporation that claims to know what it is doing and to be conducting itself properly can still give two different versions of the same story. Corporate consistency, therefore, is critical to success in socioscientific cases from the moment the first government investigator enters the picture—probably long before anyone can know that the matter is to mature into a cause célèbre. The corporation may well change its policies and approaches as science discovers new information or as social values or conditions change; it may admit that it erred in its judgment; but ordinarily it cannot change its statement of the facts without serious risk.

"Well and good," the consumer advocate responds, often most effectively in court when seeking the imposition of punitive damages (and legal fees, until the Supreme Court stated a contrary rule in federal cases), "the answer is simple enough—tell the truth. If the corporation had told the truth throughout, there would be no inconsistency today." Fair enough. Certainly a change in the corporation's perception of "truth" demands explanation. The trouble so often is that there *hasn't* been any change in that perception; it is simply that no one bothered to confirm it when the dispute began, and statements were made by corporate employees, including attorneys, which were uninformed and inaccurate because no one had troubled to conduct the required research.

The key issues in socioscientific cases don't turn on the traditional "facts"—how high is the building, how many people are employed by the corporation, how old is the first vice-president. Errors in these areas can rather easily be explained away as resulting from inadvertent mistake, or as made by an employee clearly unauthorized to speak for the company. The major issues instead involve corporate policy and corporate purpose or intent: Was the corporate purpose to meet competition, or to gain a competitive "edge." To allocate fairly, or to maintain a market position? To reward excellence, or to discriminate?

The modern large corporation is made up of thousands of employees working in many different locations, each doing a small part of the overall job. Decisions are made in bits and pieces, at different levels of operation and management. Although for most purposes the law equates a corporation with a "person," in fact, of course, the corporation itself is a strict legal fiction insofar as motivation is concerned. Its "intent" or "purpose" or "policy" is the sum total of all its parts. Sometimes, on very rare occasions, there will be a specific announcement of policy by the board of directors or chief executive, but even then it may not accord with reality. The board may have adopted and circulated a positive mandate that there be no corporate "intent to monopolize," for example, and every employee may honestly believe that he or she is acting in accord with that policy. But if conduct shows intent to monopolize, guilt will still be found.

The need to discover the corporate "story" is of great importance, and an example may be useful. Toxicological evaluation is a delicate and uncertain science, requiring difficult judgments as to just how much investigation is needed to ensure that a product does not present a significant hazard. There is no limit to the work which might be done: testing for fifty years doesn't guarantee that something won't happen in seventy-five; checking six generations doesn't forecast beyond a doubt what will happen in the seventh. But obviously choices must be made and decisions rendered for modern society to advance. Someone had to conclude that use of the Salk vaccine was justified, even if uncertainties still existed and even if something better could come along later. The alternative was to let thousands of people suffer and die.

Toxicologists working in the company's toxicology laboratory will of course make judgments different from those of corporate medical personnel concerned with treating patients, or of executives concerned with the ordering of priorities. The toxicologist who has completed initial research for a limited period with regard to one generation of one species, employing one route of administration and analyzing effects on only a few organs and one route of excretion, may conceptually and intellectually want to pursue research for a much longer period in several generations of additional species, employing different routes of administration and analyzing effects on a number of additional organs and routes of excretion. The medical doctor, on the other hand, may want the product available immediately for experimental evaluation. The executive in charge of research may be concerned that the laboratory facilities and talent devoted to the seemingly never-ending project are obstructing other much-needed research into new areas, or with respect to important epidemiological data needed to evaluate hazards suspected in an existing product.

Unless these people are carefully trained, each may give a different answer to the government investigator conducting a preliminary inquiry. The toxicologist may respond that until work is concluded, the risks of human exposure must be regarded as unacceptable, or at least that he or she cannot evaluate toxicity at this point. The doctor may say that keeping the product in the laboratory any longer is creating an unreasonable obstacle to the medical treatment of people who are seriously ill. The executive will say that use of laboratory facilities in this fashion represents a social and economic waste. No one even knows, perhaps including the investigator, whether the ultimate issue will be that an "unsafe" product was prematurely marketed; or that a "safe" product was kept off the market, resulting in unreasonable injury to those continuing to use a less-safe product; or something else altogether. Nor is it known whether the litigation context will be a government regulatory proceeding, an antitrust prosecution, a products liability case, or a stockholder derivative or class action. But the statements made will constitute telling "admissions," fully admissible in evidence at any later trial as exceptions to the hearsay rule.

Nor is it possible at this stage to know what is corporate "truth." None of these individuals is the corporation and, more likely than not, whatever corporate action was taken was the result of a number of implicit decisions rather than explicit judgments made after consideration of all the details. The only way in which the valid corporate perception can be determined is by studying all the relevant documents, speaking with all the concerned personnel, analyzing applicable corporate history and policy, and accumulating whatever other information may bear on the matter. Always the jigsaw puzzle will begin to make sense as the bits and pieces fit together, and the corporate story will emerge. Except in those rare cases where there has been fabrication, the parts will be consistent, albeit requiring explanation: The toxicologist will have been overruled, and his or her desire for additional work judged to have been more out of scientific curiosity than for needed hazard evaluation; the medical doctor's judgment that human experiment was appropriate will have been sustained, but only in limited respects and under the most controlled conditions; the executive's concern with the allocation of resources will have been resolved by a management decision to construct additional facilities and train more personnel. Whether this will "win" or "lose" whatever case is brought is still another question, but the story will be consistent from beginning to end.

It is the function of corporate counsel to prevent company personnel from making premature and uninformed statements in these early stages and to conduct the necessary factual investigation just as soon as the need becomes apparent. The first of these assignments requires a company training program, directed to those persons most likely to be in contact with potential adversaries. One cannot simply instruct them to keep silent; highly trained professionals won't accept that. Moreover, such a secrecy policy would generate doubt and suspicion among third persons with whom they deal, and quite probably result in unnecessary antagonism and litigation. This first assignment (the training program) will be dealt with later in this chapter.

The second of these assignments, thorough investigation of the facts, cannot practically be undertaken the moment the first adversary question is asked, of course. One may not even immediately recognize what is "adversarial," and the anticipated adversary may not know it either. But one can and must withhold expression of the corporate response until sufficient investigation has been completed to be certain of its validity.

The need for truthful consistency, without contrivance, is by far the most important reason for the early investigation of socioscientific litigation, but there are several other reasons. Settlement (to be discussed in detail in Chapter 5) or other disposition without trial is much easier to achieve at the beginning, when adversary counsel has not yet entered the picture and before the other side has undertaken its own lengthy investigation and gained access to information it considers damaging to the corporation. A sound settlement of course requires that one know one's own case, including potential serious deficiencies. One may even decide that a prompt application for a declaratory judgment is necessary to limit corporate exposure or risk, or that the case is so bad that one should promptly withdraw from marketing the product involved.

Evidence is also more readily accessible at the inception, before people have moved away, records are lost or destroyed, or buildings constructed or torn down. The closer one can get to the time of the event—what trial lawyers call the *res gestae*—the better. Witnesses will give their names and addresses and even volunteer statements immediately following an automobile accident, but try and approach them a few hours later!

In addition, although it approaches the province of the trial lawyer, this early investigation permits one to discover any affirmative information available on behalf of the company and concentrate on its presentation, as well as to determine company objectives and direct the controversy along what appear to be the most favorable lines. These two rules of litigation will be discussed in more detail in Chapter 6, but they should guide corporate counsel from the beginning.

Early investigation also makes possible the most rapid disposition of the controversy, whether by litigation or otherwise. Delay is not only expensive (there's an old trial lawyer's rule that one fills up time with work), but is quite generally a poor litigation tactic. Aggressive, affirmative action is consistent with a conviction in the merits of one's case, and makes possible calling the shots and keeping one's adversary off balance, *if* one is prepared. (Such straightforward effective advocacy is a quite proper function of the trial lawyer, and is *not* application of the game approach).

There are exceptions, but in general I believe in getting a case moving and over with at the earliest reasonable time.

Finally, proper early preparation can save a great deal of effort and money in other respects. The usual piecemeal approach to dealing with preliminary investigations requires search and research of the same files over and over, interrogation and reinterrogation of the same witnesses, reassignment of staff counsel, refreshment of recollection every time a new question is asked, and then repeating it all when the litigation finally materializes. How much more efficient to assign a single staff counsel to be in charge throughout, assemble all the documents and question all the witnesses as thoroughly as possible at one time and be done with it.

Where the initial inquiry does not justify this extensive an effort, a litigation plan should be settled on to apply throughout in order to minimize duplication and waste. Information can then be funnelled into a uniform retrieval and control system (also to be discussed later in this chapter), obviating the need to retrace one's steps, and witnesses, even if seen a second or third time, will not be asked the same questions repeatedly. The rewards of such organization can be substantial.

The "Team" Approach

One of the most effective approaches to preparation of socioscientific litigation is through use of a litigation team composed of all applicable corporate specialties. Depending on the case and circumstances, the team will include the staff attorney, marketing and manufacturing personnel, professionals in the relevant scientific disciplines, someone from "public information," and others as indicated. The trial lawyer should of course become a member just as soon as he or she enters the picture, but ordinarily organization of the team will have preceded the retainer.

The persons selected should be as intimately acquainted with the facts and issues as possible, should be able to devote as much time to their assignment as required, and should stay with the matter until its conclusion. Ordinarily they will not yet be the key decision makers—those individuals generally do not have sufficient time to devote to the problems—but they must have authority to speak for those executives. Ultimately they may well become key decision makers because of the expertise they acquire, and they should therefore be acceptable candidates for such positions. They should have the confidence of their colleagues and be able to tap the talents of others in seeing that necessary work is accomplished.

The function of the team is to marshal the corporation's resources in the litigation and all related matters, and to manage this aspect of the corporation's business. To do this, it must of course be fully informed in all aspects. Thus, for example, the team will not only decide whether an expensive, computerized data-retrieval system is needed to handle the documents required for the litigation itself, but whether recommendation should be made that the company discontinue the line of business involved, or undertake new, long-range environmental research and studies. These are not litigating issues as such but are total corporate matters, requiring as intimate a knowledge of the financial, production, sales, and general management specialties as of law and litigation. Accordingly, the staff attorney need not be the team chairperson or leader; in some respects it is preferable that he or she not be, because of the rather common feeling among technical and scientific personnel that lawyers are taking over in areas beyond their expertise—partially true. In larger cases, the leader of the team might be a corporate employee assigned full time to this kind of work generally, or possibly assigned to the single case as "project manager." In other cases, one would expect that the senior member of the team would act in that capacity.

The team approach benefits the corporation generally as well as its corporate counsel specifically. It assures that all relevant considerations will be brought to bear on these important matters, which extend to the full range of modern societal problems. Equally important, the team approach ensures communication of this information to the many disciplines and specialties involved, so that the final recommendation will not reflect the narrow perception of any particular viewpoint.

The team functions as an extension of corporate counsel's arms and legs, as well as eyes and ears. Staff counsel has access to whatever personnel of the corporation are required to assist in his or her functions, and need not personally read through every file or inquire into every fact. He or she can thus devote time to the legal analysis and judgment for which staff counsel has been so carefully trained.

This latter feature of the team approach deserves some emphasis. Corporate counsel, and law firms, often have great difficulty retaining good attorneys, who get sick and tired of doing work they regard as unprofessional. Once the issues have been defined by counsel, the determination of "relevance" is a logical assignment which can be carried out by anyone with intelligence and the needed specific background; it does not require law-school education. Attorneys must certainly oversee the effort, but the employment of attorneys in the selection, digesting, and indexing of huge masses of documents is a massive waste of resources. Law firms have learned this, and are using paralegals in ever greater numbers. The paralegal function in this regard does not require the specialized training given to those who prepare drafts of wills and court pleadings, and handle a multitude of other truly quasi-legal assignments. The use of the team approach, rendering pertinent personnel throughout the entire corporation team participants and, in effect, paralegal aids to the law department, is entirely possible, and will be an important aid to corporate counsel in maintaining and upgrading the quality of his or her legal staff.

Use of the team approach, and through it all of the other resources of the corporation, obviously also saves substantial litigation expense—law-firm paralegal help runs as high today as $25 per hour and sometimes more. But it has another and in some respects most important benefit—it helps educate corporate personnel generally, as well as in the litigation itself. The key to sound witness preparation is full knowledge of the facts and issues;

the members of the litigation team, and those working with them, receive this kind of education from the moment they begin to work on the suit. And apart from their roles as witnesses in this and other cases, corporate personnel generally begin vigilantly to view their present actions as they will appear in a future litigation context. They soon recognize how dangerous the off-the-cuff comment or the ill-considered document can be; the need to be continually aware that all actions, statements, and conduct must be able to withstand the most critical subsequent examination and attack by the most extreme adversary. This kind of educational effort over the long run will reduce the corporation's litigation exposure immeasurably.

From the point of view of the litigation alone, the team approach makes possible an essential interaction between science and law. Socioscientific cases are legal cases only in the narrowest of senses. They are in truth social, scientific, *and* legal cases. The lawyers involved must do their best to understand all the esoteric specialties involved, but they obviously cannot know as much as the professionals in the necessary disciplines. The attorney requires the talent of the expert even to frame the relevant technological issues germane to the case, and as a resource and equal partner in the structuring of the litigation. There must be effective communication between scientific expert and attorney, with a high degree of continued interaction between them at all stages of the litigation process. Each must understand the other's goals, methodologies, and limitations, a situation that cannot exist if the expert is brought into the case only on an ad hoc basis for consultation as problems arise, as testimony is required, or as some other gap needs emergency filling. In addition, as discussed later in this chapter, this close interaction is essential to the effective testimony of the scientist. Its absence contributes to science's disenchantment with the adversary process as presently practiced.

Finally, the team approach enormously enhances the ability to examine conduct from the perspective of others, a key requirement of the rule of reason. A person with grey hair may be able to understand the views of the younger generation, but it helps to have a junior on the team, or a representative of a minority group affected. It isn't enough simply to ask such a person how a proposed corporate policy statement will sound—the respondent can fully answer only if he or she is an intimate participant, who knows all the details. (This analysis has far broader implications to the modern corporation, of course. It encourages boards of directors, for example, to seek a broad spectrum of views and interests from directors, so as to be best able to formulate policies consistent with a standard of conduct acceptable to society overall.)

The team approach is not easy. Colonel Lindbergh is said to have replied when he was congratulated for having flown the Atlantic Ocean "all alone": "It would have been a lot tougher with a committee!" Lawyers are often "loners," and resist giving up any part of their perceived independence and jurisdiction. They must be made to learn the many advantages of the team approach, for there is no other way to deal adequately and properly with the great problems of the modern socioscientific case.

Litigation Ethics

The next sections of this chapter will deal with the specific tasks that must be undertaken to complete the "thorough investigation of the facts" required for effective pretrial preparation. But there is an important preliminary question which must be answered before the work begins: "What if the investigation turns up information that is seriously damaging?"

The answer may be simple enough to the layperson. It is to withdraw, settle, admit error, or do whatever else is possible to achieve the best result in light of the facts. But this is not necessarily the response of the trial attorney. Our litigation system requires that a lawyer achieve the best result possible for the client in the specific assignment for which he or she has been retained, provided that no violation of the law or the ethics of the legal profession is involved. Any "seriously damaging" information developed may be known only to a witness now deceased, or contained in a privileged document which need not be disclosed. The evidence will thus not get into the hands of the present adversary. The trial attorney can "win" the litigation, properly and lawfully, even though the case as presented is by no means the whole truth.

The dilemma in which this sometimes places trial lawyers is not theoretical. One law professor identified the three most serious questions which result as follows:

1. Is it proper to cross-examine for the purpose of discrediting the reliability or the credibility of an adverse witness whom you know to be telling the truth?

2. Is it proper to put on the stand a witness whom you know will commit perjury?

3. Is it proper to give your client legal advice when you have reason to believe that the knowledge you give him will tempt him to commit perjury? *

This educator's answer was "that there are policy considerations that at times justify frustrating the search for truth and the prosecution of a just claim. So, too, there are policies that justify an affirmative answer to the three questions that I have posed." †

Lawyers like these answers no more than the layperson. They understand the policy considerations which call for the result; yet they are repelled by the need to participate in what is so clearly an unhappy assignment. Frequently they avoid the problem by procedures that are at best disingenuous: "Don't tell me about that"; "If a document of that kind still exists, we'll lose the case," with a knowing look suggesting that such a document should not be disclosed; "If you crossed the street against the light, you'll lose the case. What color was the light when you crossed?"; "You have

---

* Freedman, "Professional Responsibility of the Criminal Defense Lawyer: The Three Hardest Questions," *New York Law Journal*, 23 August 1966, p. 1; see also Freedman, *Lawyers' Ethics in an Adversary System* (Indianapolis: Bobbs-Merrill, 1975).

† Ibid., 24 August 1966, p. 4.

two alternatives—either shape up and testify properly, or check into a hospital until the case is over." Such conduct is worse than the alternatives avoided. It seeks to shift the blame solely to the client, making the attorney appear as an innocent party. It adds self-preservation and consciousness of wrongdoing to whatever other improprieties may be felt. The lawyer should know better.

The rule-of-reason response to these questions is straightforward and simple. It looks to the long range, not the specific and limited representation or case presented. It knows that the short-run "win" can mean defeat overall. It recognizes that the dangers of suppression and concealment are too great to accept: too many people are involved, too long a time, too many issues. Somehow, somewhere "the truth will out." It demands no fine balancing of competing ethical considerations. It requires that the case be prepared and presented in light of the truth as it can best be ascertained. This calls for different approaches in different circumstances, to be discussed as they arise throughout this book. But in all cases the rule of reason insists that stated litigation posture be consistent with the truth, whether disclosed or not, and that the truth never be embarrassing or damaging to credibility if revealed. It may result in a poor settlement or loss of the case in total, but corporate credibility will remain intact. This is the only way in which such cases can be handled successfully over the long run, for the many reasons already indicated. The resulting ethical satisfaction is what makes the process augur so well for the future of our system of justice.

The Document Search

The corporate legal department is rarely involved in a dispute of its own. Ordinarily its participation will have been triggered by a communication from another department which has or anticipates a problem, or in response to routine legal surveys seeking to uncover questionable areas. Whatever the source, however, in almost all cases the initial report will tell only a small part of the story. And because we are all so much the victims of our own perceptions, more commonly than not the report will characterize the complaint as that of a "crank," or otherwise assure that the company's case is a good one. There are alarmists and doom-anticipators, of course, and their presentations will be equally unrealistic. Only very infrequently does the first discussion or interview with a client satisfactorily evaluate the merits. Corporate counsel's function at this point must be to go out and dig up the facts, a process requiring examination of documents and discussions with the personnel involved.

Document inspection and witness interview can occur in any order or simultaneously, but where there are no time constraints, examination of the important documents should come first. A document may be misleading or inaccurate, but it is a permanent part of the record and must be dealt with throughout the matter. Witness recollections and perceptions, in contrast, will change quite radically as recollections are refreshed and additional considerations uncovered. Furthermore, because both must be undertaken in any event, it saves the witnesses time if corporate counsel comes to the first sessions knowledgeable in background information and able to ask the witnesses probing and difficult questions. In cases where corporate counsel has no technical background at all, it may be desirable to confer with technical specialists to clarify the documents; usually, however, enough of this expertise will have been furnished in the initial report disclosing the problem.

Obviously until the matter has been evaluated as one justifying a full litigation effort, the document search should be geared to the limits of the problem presented (with the materials processed in such a fashion as to avoid duplication and waste). But sooner or later in the socioscientific case, before or after the final claim has been presented and the litigation commenced, it will be necessary to assemble *all* the relevant documents. Although trial counsel should participate in the supervision of this effort as soon as he or she has been retained, I regard this activity as the prime responsibility of corporate counsel. He or she must see to it that the people actually conducting the search understand that a "document" means anything that may be a record of the event, from paper, to recording, to computer run, to photograph, and even to tombstone, copies as well as originals; they must know what they are looking for and undertake the necessary inspections to find it; they must not make judgments as to what is "good" or "bad," or destroy or suppress anything (evidence of the latter can be far more damaging than anything suppressed, and more than likely they will have destroyed a useful explanation anyway!).

Exhibit 1 illustrates the kind of carefully written instructions which should be given, to be followed by meetings and consultations. Because people will misunderstand no matter how careful the instructions, corporate counsel should maintain continuing routine supervision to be sure that instructions are being carried out properly.

EXHIBIT I
DOCUMENT SEARCH INSTRUCTIONS

CONFIDENTIAL—FOR LITIGATION USE ONLY

UNDER NO CIRCUMSTANCES SHOULD ANYONE IN ANY WAY SUPPRESS, DESTROY, DOCTOR, OR TAMPER WITH A DOCUMENT. TO DO SO WOULD NOT ONLY BE UNETHICAL, IMMORAL, AND PERHAPS UNLAWFUL, BUT WOULD CERTAINLY HURT OUR CASE. THE COMPANY IS RELYING FOR JUSTICE ON THE TRUTH OF WHAT HAPPENED. WE DO NOT HAVE TO SHADE THAT TRUTH ONE IOTA. EVEN IF YOU THINK SOMETHING IS HARMFUL AND SHOULD BE CORRECTED, PLEASE DISCUSS EVERYTHING FULLY AND FRANKLY WITH US.

DEFINITIONS

1. We are looking for "documents." A document is not just a letter or a contract. It is anything that is a record, such as a computer run, a sales slip, handwritten notes, a diary, a photograph, a cancelled check, a page of a book of account, a tape recording, and even a computer memory or a stone tablet.

2. The word "document" includes records you consider harmful as well as those you consider helpful. If there is anything you think may be embarrassing (and you could well be wrong), we certainly ought to know about it before any of our people testify.

3. At this point, we are simply trying to define our problem so that we can know how to proceed. We lawyers know that the documents involved are very voluminous, and might even be impossible to produce without going out of business. We are looking for information and help from you to lick this problem and still win the case, not trying to make work. We also know about vacation and holiday schedules. The only way we can decide how to handle this problem is to know what there is. Then we will be able to recommend a course of action.

4. We are looking for any document in the possession of the company or any of its related companies, or under its control. By "related companies" we mean subsidiaries, affiliates, or predecessors. By "control" we mean records owned by the company but in the physical custody of agents or employees, such as lawyers, accountants, or executives. This does not include, however, records that belong personally to an executive or representative. We are not being technical, and want to turn up anything we can, wherever located.

5. We are not asking for nonexistent documents, such as records that have been destroyed, or for records in the possession of other predecessor companies no longer under our control, or special summaries of income or expenses made up from existing books, etc. (We may ask for some of these later.)

6. Usually we will want the original record, not a copy. An obvious exception is a computer record, in which case we do not want either the electronic memory, the punched cards, or the first run, but rather the first final accounting record made from the initial run or from work sheets. However, we also want copies of documents that differ in any way from the original, whether because of some handwritten interlineation, such as underscoring or notes, or date stamp, or receipt or file stamp or notation which indicates that somebody other than the sender or recipient received or read the document.

7. We are looking for all documents "relevant" to our case in any way, even documents not within the requests given to us or

ones that we will not furnish. The reason we want to cover everything now is to avoid coming back a second time and reviewing the same files again each time we receive additional requests from any of the parties, or when we need documents for our own use to refresh somebody's memory, or to introduce in evidence at trial. Only those having complete knowledge of the case can know what is "relevant," so do not proceed with any searches without specific instruction.

8. There is very great time pressure to complete our task. This pressure is our own doing, because the company is struggling to preserve its right to be in business and any delay necessarily is a delay in getting its day in court.

DOCUMENTS NEEDED

The following list of types of documents sought is not meant to be all inclusive. We lawyers intend to meet with each of you promptly, because we do not know how you keep your records or what kinds of documents you have. There will undoubtedly be a great many other types of relevant records disclosed after we have talked. These categories were drafted based only upon our own guess as to what exists.

1. Financial records given to the public, including annual and quarterly reports, stockholder letters, SEC prospectuses and the like.

2. Formal corporate records such as minutes, charters, certificates of incorporation and bylaws, and amendments.

3. Documents filed with federal and state agencies, such as income- and excise-tax returns, sales- and use-tax returns, and the like.

4. Sales documents relating to the company's products, including sales literature, correspondence and bulletins to sales personnel, correspondence and memoranda with customers, orders, delivery instructions, etc.

5. Records, financial or otherwise, dealing with the success or failure of the company's business, showing expenses, income, potential, production.

6. Engineering and technical records relating to design and production.

7. Records dealing in any way with attempts to develop alternative courses of marketing action, whether successful or unsuccessful.

8. Records dealing with financing of supply and sales, whether foreign or domestic, including correspondence of any kind with brokers and dealers or banks, market reports, credit analyses of distributors and dealers, and general credit problems with distributors and dealers.

9. General forms in use by the Company with outsiders such as customers or independent salesmen or suppliers, including standard order forms, standard sales forms, and the like.

10. Service problems and complaints and their remedy.

11. Documents passing between the company and any affiliated company and the SEC or the New York Stock Exchange.

12. Documents passing between the company and the other parties or any of their affiliates.

13. Anything else you think is relevant or helpful or harmful to our case.

Something must be done with the documents obtained, of course, and a system must be designed to assure their proper handling and retrieval. If all documents are simply dumped in some central file, it may be impossible to later know which came from where, and source can be crucial evidence ("Did Jones see this at the time"). Even the order of documents in an original file can be significant as indicating chronological sequence of receipt or mailing, or whether something was attached to or enclosed with something else. Many files will be current ones, needed for the company's on-going business, or for a tax examination or other continuing problem and cannot be removed from their remote locations. There are many ways of handling these various problems, such as by indexing, microfilming, or other duplication, but some uniform procedure should be adopted which will apply throughout the litigation.

Information retrieval presents even more difficult problems in the major cases, because there is no way of initially knowing just what will be required and when. Issues will inevitably be refined and probably changed as the litigation develops. Some system that will permit one to find whatever is later required—by person or organization involved, by subject matter (frequently termed "witness" and "subject matter" files), and by chronology—is needed. The system must fit present needs and also be expandable as the litigation changes and grows. Again, numerous methods are available, including the use of computerized retrieval techniques.

Two comments are appropriate. First, experts in document administration and retrieval methods quite probably are in the employ of the corporation itself. It is difficult to understand why lawyers so often think they must develop their own techniques, "reinvent the wheel," as it were, when technically qualified personnel are at hand. Corporate counsel's responsibility should be to consult with in-house experts, or go outside if necessary, to come up with a filing and retrieval system geared to the business and facilities of the corporation and the short- and long-term needs of the legal department.

Second, it is also difficult to understand why attorneys in even the largest corporations use such antiquated methods, when their business colleagues have the most modern and advanced communication, filing, reproduction, and electronic data-processing techniques. Some of this will be discussed later in the chapter under "Internal Management and Control." Here it must be pointed out that a law department's search through loosely fastened, unwieldly files is an anachronism that cannot be justified when the department next door can obtain almost instant access to the same information by typing a few numbers or letters on a terminal keyboard and viewing a screen, or by obtaining computer output from a microfilm. Where any significant continuing number of important socioscientific litigations can be anticipated, corporate counsel should ask the experts to design a system of general application, useful over the years, into which all such materials can be channeled. It will certainly take education and adjustment in the beginning, but the attorneys will inevitably welcome it. And once again, the cost savings will be enormous.

Litigators skilled in the old school may oppose the use of modern retrieval methods on the grounds that an adversary's task in discovery will be that much easier. This may be a consequence, of course; it is even possible in some jurisdictions that an adversary may get access to the system itself and thereby find out what questions to ask. But this is a small price to pay for the benefits gained. The greatest danger to the corporate client in socioscientific litigation is *not* knowing the facts. If the choice is between knowledge by both sides (which it is not—I consider the objection exaggerated) or not at all, the decision must be for the former.

Currently a kind of "Watergate Syndrome" seems to be prevalent, urging that corporations adopt policies mandating the earliest possible destruction of corporate records, again to prevent their inspection by adversaries. I believe this is an unfortunate overreaction to the disclosure of the White House tapes, and that any harm which might result from expedited adversary discovery is far outbalanced by the advantage of having access to the facts to refresh memories and set the record straight. In another and quite unrelated connection, sometimes documents appearing to be worthless turn out to have great fall-out value, as in the case of medical records that become useful in subsequent epidemiological research. As a general rule, if you are trying to do the right thing and are reasonably capable, retained files are more likely to help your cause than hurt it.

The only reason for document destruction should be to eliminate the waste of space and related time and money resulting from the accumulation of large numbers of records over the years. Any corporate procedure in this regard should be a general one, to avoid any suggestion that specific documents are being destroyed for evidentiary purposes. The procedure should be termed a "file preservation" rather than a "file destruction" policy, to make its purpose clear.

Privilege

The use of the team approach and of so many nonlegal corporate personnel to assist in the legal preparation necessarily in-
creases concern that attorney-client privilege and "work product"
and trade-secret protection will be jeopardized. The rule of reason does not contemplate waiving either of these important rights
in the name of full disclosure. Both are socially as well as legally
approved, and necessary to proper conduct of the company's business; both can be explained to a lay arbiter and public as not
inconsistent with credibility. Accordingly, special care to maximize
their availability is required in the corporate legal department administering socioscientific litigations.

First, as to attorney-client privilege: Where a communication
falls within its confines, it is absolutely protected from disclosure
(except on review by a court to determine whether the privilege
in fact exists, an important exception which means in practical
application that even here internal inconsistency can be uncovered). The traditional definition of Professor Wigmore (still the
leading authority on evidence) is applied in different ways in different jurisdictions, and the extent to which corporate communications are protected has been considerably attenuated in some. But
the privilege does exist, and judges, who are of course lawyers
themselves, usually go out of their way to protect confidential
communications between attorney and client, even if such communications don't fall within the strict letter of the Wigmore
text. The confidential character of the message, as between attorney and client, is always at the heart of the privilege. With
so many documents involved in the large socioscientific case, so
many people participating in the rule-of-reason team corporate
approach, and duplication and the sending of "information" copies
so much in vogue generally, the essential confidentiality is necessarily suspect. Moreover, unless precautions are taken, paralegal
personnel reviewing papers years after they were prepared are
hard put to know who was and who was not an attorney or cor-

porate employee with sufficient participation in the matter to justify the appellation "client," so that privilege might apply.

Both general and special measures are required to deal with this problem. Generally, corporate counsel should design stationery that identifies the source of any document as the legal department. Attorneys should type in a title after their names; simply "Attorney, Jones Company" will do if corporate counsel prefers a minimum of hierarchical titles. It should be clear policy that copies of internal privileged documents will not be broadcast wholesale as is so often the case, and should be circulated only on a "need to know" basis. In special cases, documents of significance should be marked "privileged," or "confidential communication from attorney to client," or "do not make copies without permission of the author," or the equivalents. Care should be taken to separate legal from business and commercial matters. Key documents, such as legal opinions evaluating alternative courses of action, might in addition be numbered and controlled, with such notations as "Copy for Mr. Smith only" or "Return to Legal Department." (It is worth emphasizing that one should never write "destroy after reading," because of the obvious negative implications incident to any suppression.)

Where practical, the legal department should encourage other involved parties in the corporation to adopt similar policies. Frequently the number of corporate personnel involved will be a relatively small subset of the corporation generally, and this will be easy to do. If too many are involved, this at least may be possible after the initiating documents in any legal matter have been received. And in any event, there should be routine processing of all documents received by the legal department, including at a minimum the use of a receipt stamp with the words "Legal Department" and the date.

Attorney "work product" is a conditional exemption from production rather than an absolute privilege. But it is difficult for an antagonist to obtain such documents in any jurisdiction without a substantial showing of unavailability of the information elsewhere without unreasonable effort and expense. As with attorney-client privilege, judges tend to want to protect the efforts of fellow professionals from what seems unfair appropriation. Once again, application of the exemption varies from place to place, but always it requires that the materials protected have been involved in the handling of a controversy or dispute. Here corporate counsel should require that all documents relating to controverted matters be marked clearly at the outset to identify the claim, such as the traditional *"Re: Water Quality Claim."* A record should be kept of all paralegal personnel working on each matter, even if serving only for a short time to conduct a limited document search. Members of the litigation team and others working with them should routinely mark everything they handle with the legal title of the matter. When practical, they should route their documents through the legal department for its information as well as to emphasize that the work is part of the litigation preparation. In larger and longer cases, stationery might be printed for use of the litigation team and its assistants; if no individual case justifies the expense, there might be stationery of general application to fill the same need.

Trade-secret exemption, like work product, is not an absolute privilege but a conditional exemption safeguarding valuable confidential commercial information. Its existence depends not only on the nature of the underlying confidence, but on the litigation context in which it arises. Even the most valuable trade secret, such as a secret production formula, for example, must be disclosed in a litigation based upon its alleged theft, although protective court orders can usually be obtained limiting employment of the information to the litigation and precluding its competitive commercial use. There is much that corporate and trial counsel can do to safeguard privilege later on in the design of the protective order, but the very existence of the exemption will depend on what has been done in the earlier stages.

As in the other cases, the application of trade-secret exemption varies by jurisdiction, but always its existence will depend partly on secrecy. A trade secret which has been publicly disclosed without restriction, even inadvertently, is no trade secret at all. Moreover, security measures adopted to prevent unauthorized disclosure also serve as evidence that the secret was developed and is owned by the company, and is considered valuable. An arbiter understandably looks with some doubt upon the all-too-common claims of business secrecy concerning information that has been broadcast widely within the company and to suppliers and customers, without even being marked "confidential" or requiring the execution of a nondisclosure agreement. Such claims necessarily impair corporate credibility.

Corporate counsel should of course guide and advise corporate employees in the development and protection of trade secrets, including the maintenance of logs recording development and cost, security measures, nondisclosure and noncompetition agreements, and the like. Special care is needed in dealing with subcontractors who must be given access to confidential information in connection with government contracts. All of this will be most useful in any contest. Even if it has been overlooked at the inception, however, corporate counsel can maximize the possibility of protection during litigation preparation. Corporate personnel should be urged to identify any confidential formula, pattern, device, or compilation of information used in the business which they believe gives the corporation an opportunity to obtain an advantage over competitors that do not have it. These may fall within traditional trade-secret classifications. If inquiry discloses that a realistic and sound argument can be made that the information is properly so classified, it should be isolated and handled with procedures designed to maintain its security, including bold security identification, placement under lock and key with restricted access and careful record keeping.

Remember, however, that laypersons generally, and business-persons in particular, do not always understand legal procedure and do not see why they should be made to disclose so much to adversaries and antagonists. They are prone to characterize almost anything as "confidential business information," including even that disclosed in prospectuses disseminated to the public. Corporate counsel has a responsibility to set the client straight and conduct the needed independent investigation in this regard, even if the client expresses reluctance. Better that it come from a friend than a foe! To claim secrecy for a document which turns out to have been publicly disclosed is both most embarrassing and an insult to credibility.

Safeguarding corporate confidences is an important aspect of corporate counsel's responsibility, but one can never rely on such security with any assurance. Work-product and trade-secret exemption are only conditional rights, lost upon the proper showing of "need to know"; attorney-client privilege does not necessarily exempt the information from review by a court, which inevitably considers what it has learned in its evaluation of the case (i.e., can a judge *really* credit witness testimony that is at odds with a privileged document that very witness wrote and which the judge has just reviewed?). The privilege is also subject to inevitable inadvertent disclosure in the "big" case involving millions of documents, as well as to the advertent disclosure referred to at the outset, resulting from the far-flung operations of the corporate litigant in the socioscientific case and the disclosures of aggrieved or extremist employees. These rights are in truth shields of protection, not swords of aggression in an adversary litigation. The need to consider one's conduct as continually "center stage" remains paramount.

Witness Interviews

Whether it comes before, after, or simultaneously with the document search, the interrogation of those persons having relevant information must be one of the early steps taken by corporate counsel in his or her investigation and preparation of the litigation. Documents are vital as permanent records; rarely, however, are the documents crucial in the socioscientific case. Usually the final issues will turn upon intent, purpose, and policy, and the balancing of a myriad of intangibles not reduced to record form.

Persons having relevant information—witnesses—may be company employees or outsiders, friendly or hostile. And these classifications will change with time in the large case with many participants. All witnesses must be seen as soon as is consistent with the needs of the investigation and a reasonable prognosis of its development. The purpose of interviewing each is initially the same—to obtain the information required to evaluate and prepare the case. Questioning should therefore be as thorough and detailed as possible, with reference where appropriate to the documents, to what others have said, or to anything else that will contribute to the fullest possible understanding. In some cases, however—for example when questioning an extremely hostile witness —such disclosure should be limited because of the probability that the witness will misuse any materials gleaned from the interview.

Dealings will vary according to categories of witnesses, but some observations are useful generally. A major objective of all interviews should be to obtain a knowledge of the probable adversary perception. Understanding one's adversary and anticipating his or her reactions and moves is one of the most important requirements in the effective handling of a litigation. Too often the litigant underestimates the adversary, concluding that he or she will "fold" on opposition, or won't prepare adequately, or is engaged in a "strike" (unjustified) suit, or is otherwise improperly motivated. More commonly, however, the adversary is just as good, just as convinced, and just as righteous; in any event, it always pays to assume this to be the case until the contrary is proven. If wrong, at worst one will be overprepared, a small price to pay for avoiding the risk of misjudgment. Asking the critical questions designed to discover "why" and "how" is therefore mandatory.

Remember also that everyone perceives differently, even witnesses employed by the company, and may later change perception. There is substantial danger in early investigations, before enough is known and a strategy developed, that others will perceive the conduct of the investigator in a very different way than intended. The complaining witness who has initiated a complaint to the Justice Department may perceive an expression of willingness to compensate for damages as an effort to bribe or obstruct justice; the company employee may view questions inquiring about the need for research as an effort to block the discovery of negative evidence; the author of an apparently damaging document may consider comment regarding its unfortunate implications as a suggestion that it should be destroyed. Those conducting the investigation should be on guard against their own conduct giving rise to additional claims of libel, slander, malicious prosecution, obstruction of justice, or restraint of trade. Careful, detailed, current memoranda should be kept, reflecting what is said and done, including purpose where pertinent. Sometimes it may even be the wisest course to limit risk and doubt by initiating declaratory judgment action, in effect soliciting the court's advice, or formally offering in court to pay the proper amount of damages. What one does and says in litigation preparation is as much a part of the record as anything else, and can be used in the most persuasive adversary fashion by an antagonist with a different perception.

Memoranda reflecting interviews should be a regular and routine part of corporate counsel's professional business—they can be used later on in the litigation and counsel can verify and even testify to them. (Memoranda should be prepared for all other events of importance as well, including internal legal-staff debates which may leave someone displeased or dissatisfied, and likely later to report a different perception of the event.) They should be phrased in sound Wigmore form, so as to be useful as either "past recollection recorded" or "present recollection revived." They should begin with the traditional language, "I am dictating immediately following my return to the office, from notes made by me during my meeting with Jones, while my recollection is still fresh and clear." After the memorandum is completed and compared with the notes, the latter should be destroyed routinely, unless there is some special reason to keep them (as when they have been shown to the witness or marked by him, as discussed later). This should also be done for friendly company witnesses in the important fact areas, for the presently friendly witness may later turn hostile. Nor should company fact preparation be dependent upon the recollection of the staff attorney in charge, who may get sick or be transferred or possibly leave the company.

Of course "friendly" interviews can leave uncertain areas for later discussion when "freezing" the recollection in a memorandum may be more appropriate. There is much room for professional discretion in approaching different kinds of witness. But solving the problem by writing nothing concerning friendly witnesses not only poses administrative obstacles to management of the litigation and creates risk, but makes it possible for an adversary to contend —with some justification—that memoranda exclusively of "unfriendly" interviews are obviously selective, slanted, and self-serving.

The Company Witness

By "company" witness, I refer to persons who in all probability can be expected to view the litigation in much the same fashion as the corporation, and who will likely be called as witnesses on its behalf. They may or may not be employees.

"Witness preparation" is a term commonly applied to that last period before a witness testifies, when he or she is furnished advice on the mechanics of the process—the need to tell the truth, what the deposition room or courtroom looks like, whether witnesses can smoke or request advice, how the adversary attorney conducts himself or herself, what kinds of question to anticipate, the importance of keeping temper, and much more. But true witness preparation in the socioscientific litigation in fact begins at the very beginning, with the underlying facts themselves. One cannot purport to prepare properly in just the few hours before testimony or trial. It is an on-going, never-ending process. Cross-examination, which will be discussed in Chapter 7, is just good, careful questioning. If the witness understands the issues, has a refreshed recollection, and is confident and comfortable by virtue of careful preparation from the beginning, he will be just fine, whatever the skills of the cross-examiner.

The company scientist who, during preliminary research, is obviously antagonistic and exhibits a determination to "win" in his or her approach to adversarial peers, will be hard put to convince the arbiter later that the rule of reason actually has been applied in his or her work and testimony. The scientist can no more avoid the damaging impact of premature evaluations or uninformed statements, or inconsistencies stated privately but later disclosed by another, than if he or she had made them in a deposition or at the trial itself.

Relations between Scientist and Attorney

Corporate counsel seeking to apply the rule of reason need to "untrain" company personnel, particularly scientists and technicians, from what they have learned of the sporting approach to litigation. The tension so often experienced by scientists who testify is the result of their being torn between their advocate's desire to present certainty and the delicate balancing of the evidence, which they know should be their scientific function. They should not plead a "cause." They should explain methodology and opinion in direct testimony, not by the more common process of backing down from absolutism during cross-examination. They should furnish a technological assessment of the limitations inherent in formulating an opinion, and communicate the assignment of realistic probabilities of alternative courses of action. It is not their job to be advocates and "win" for the corporation.

When a scientist testifies: "The risk is acceptable," he is expressing a view made up of scientific observation, scientific analysis, and scientific opinion, which often are not seriously disputed,*

---

* This is why the proposal for a "science court," composed of highly qualified scientists, to decide purely scientific issues, deals with only a part of the problem in these cases, and probably the lesser one at that. Better not to tamper with the "scientific method" for deciding such issues, including peer review, which has worked so well.

and personal evaluation and conclusion, the differences in which are the ultimate issue in the litigation. Usually these components are confused subconsciously or unwittingly; sometimes they are confused to buffalo the layperson. In either case, the result is the battle of scientific experts so common to the socioscientific litigation, a conflict which has led to disenchantment by layperson and scientist alike and has seriously impaired the credibility of all the parties involved. But it is the corporate party which suffers the most, because its personality and presence carry over from case to case while the opposition shifts.

The witness training program and "unlearning" process should be an on-going corporate program for those employees anticipated to be involved in socio-scientific litigations, and an early part of witness preparation for those nonemployee company witnesses who have not been subjected to it. In both cases it should be the same: Corporate counsel should explain the function of the witness as here outlined, and make clear that the witness's total conduct will be used to judge the validity of his or her testimony. The witness must not make light and unguarded "private" or "off-the-record" statements that suggest the truth to be something different than trial testimony, nor pretend to knowledge that he or she does not have, such as corporate purpose or intent. The witness should not render premature evaluations and representations before the needed facts are in. He or she must not take on the trial lawyer's role and become a part of the adversary process, revealing a bias and prejudice in his or her work which is inconsistent with the alleged scientific method.

This last requirement will be particularly difficult for the employee to accept and follow, because it is so very different from present procedures. It means, for example, that the witness must answer letters or speak with hostile scientists and either respond to their legitimate questions or explain why not. He or she cannot withhold, for the purpose of "sandbagging" and springing on an adversary at the propitious moment on cross-examination, important new research which accepted professional practice requires be disclosed and subjected to peer review. He or she cannot conceal what may be considered unhelpful, nor play adversary "tricks." The witness cannot in any way display prejudice and bias, and must strive mightily to avoid these human emotions. We are part of a society that is developing new rules to govern itself democratically, rules which require that *all* differences be considered. Someone who values organic foods to the point of wanting to outlaw pesticides is not "bad," but simply may not understand or appreciate the need to feed the populations of the world. Such an opponent can be defeated only by reason and evidence, not bias and hostility.

When a company witness is in doubt as to how to act and the litigation is in progress, he or she may certainly express the wish to speak with corporate counsel. In some cases the witness should even be instructed to do so. But this is not usually possible while the facts are developing and before a dispute has arisen, and in any event does inject the adversary process into the picture at a time when credibility would be enhanced by an immediate and affirmative response. Action taken after delay occasioned by the need to consult with counsel may well be perceived as "self-serving." A general witness training program is accordingly the best long-range way to instill the appropriate attitudes.

Two other items should be emphasized in the interviews with company witnesses—the need to develop and present an affirmative, positive approach; and the need to simplify the complex and difficult to the maximum possible extent. Both are valuable in connection with preparation of the litigation generally and as a part of witness preparation.

An affirmative approach is essential to effective advocacy. The government need not prove motive in the criminal case, but rarely obtains a conviction if it cannot show why the defendant acted as he did; the defense need only watch the state fail to prove all necessary elements of the case beyond a reasonable doubt, but acquittal is rare if the defendant doesn't have an alibi or, in Perry Mason fashion, show "who done it." As aptly expressed in a popular song of the forties: "You've got to accentuate the positive, eliminate the negative, don't mess with Mr. In-between."

All of this is especially true in the present spate of socio-scientific litigations, with environmental and consumerism causes in such high public favor and corporate credibility in such low esteem. Yet although these are all in one fashion or another "risk/*benefit*" cases, corporate participation often foolishly accepts the challenge on the ground presented—the risk—without emphasizing or sometimes even presenting the affirmative—the benefit.

Proper evaluation of the hazard or risk charged is, of course, an important part of the corporation's case. But in early discussions corporate counsel should press the witnesses to begin thinking along "benefit" lines as well, and preferably not in strictly economic terms. How much food will be produced? How many jobs created? How many lives saved? The public is willing to accept a guaranteed 50,000–60,000 deaths per year from automobile accidents in this country because it understands the benefits of automotive travel; it will do the same for other far lower degrees of hazard if the even greater comparative benefits are properly explained.

Witnesses should be advised also to emphasize these benefits in all their presentations, and corporate counsel should see that the same is done in all other litigation contexts as well, including briefs and oral arguments. A judge will be much less likely to enter a temporary restraining order preventing suffering patients from obtaining a needed drug if its *affirmative* benefit is emphasized, than if told only of the inadequacy of the evaluation of suspected teratogenicity.

The need to communicate effectively to laypersons must also be emphasized in company witness discussions. *Total* lay understanding is impossible, of course; otherwise the expertise of the specialist would not be so critical. But some information can always be communicated satisfactorily. The sensitive heart surgeon does answer the patient's questions and explain as much as he or she can. And the lay mind works in a peculiar way; if it has understood and accepted some of the esoteric considerations and grasped a part of the technical language, it extrapolates to the balance and accepts the whole. If the analytical chemist takes pains to explain what a "part per trillion" means in comparative terms ("the equivalent of one drop of vermouth in so many car-loads of gin"), the difficulty in distinguishing gas chromatographic signals at such extremely low levels from background noise and other interferences, and the problems involved in obtaining clean equipment and samples, perhaps using charts, physical equipment, and demonstrations, the audience will much more readily accept the chemist's conclusion regarding the analysis and its significance even though the two are not strictly related.

Corporate counsel, and later trial counsel, will of course have to learn as much of the specialty involved as necessary to participate with the witnesses in the communication process. But this is no unpleasant task. Instead it is one of the exciting and rewarding aspects of trial law, granting the attorney an opportunity to be educated by the most outstanding teachers. The communication measures and tools developed will be as useful to counsel in explaining the case to the arbiter as they are to the witnesses. And the sooner counsel can begin that education, the more credible it will appear (i.e., not simply a trial lawyer's clever tactic), and the more the arbiter educational process will have been reinforced by the time trial begins.

Scientists often need more careful and intensive preparation than less technically specialized executives and managers. They are not as accustomed to modifying approaches to adjust to the perceptions of others, as the salesman must; or to having their positive statements doubted; or to having their motivations questioned. For these reasons, attacks on them by cross-examiners are sometimes far more aggressive and antagonistic than those on lay witnesses whose financial motivations are obvious and even admitted. Despite this, experience teaches that company technical witnesses trained in these new techniques of the rule-of-reason approach become enthusiastic advocates of the system, ever more convinced of the soundness and integrity of their case and the morality of their corporate employer. Even the scientists no longer fear trial and cross-examination; they almost welcome it. Such a change in attitude is a pleasure to behold.

One other comment about company witnesses. With rare exception, a bad witness is almost always the fault of the attorney, not of the individual. An assembly-line worker may not be as intelligent or experienced as a director of research, but should be able to come through for what he or she is. It requires work to achieve this training, however, in some cases including repeated discussions, brutal mock cross-examinations, instructions from top management to follow advice, and perhaps even preliminary comment to the court or jury anticipating the problem areas. But I perspire far more freely when witnesses I have called testify on direct examination than when I cross-examine, for they are my responsibility. If they fail, I have failed them and the client as well.

The Hostile Witness

By "hostile" witnesses, I refer to persons who are expected to view the litigation in the same fashion as the corporation's anticipated adversary. They are not necessarily antagonistic at this early point, although they are of course likely to be so. Usually they are third parties, but sometimes even employees will be hostile witnesses.

The purpose in interviewing hostile witnesses is the same as in interviewing the friendly—to obtain the information required to evaluate and prepare the case. But because the antagonism incident to the "game" approach is so common, here the two interview processes often part company.

Sometimes, of course, a hostile witness will be agreeable to conferring. The earlier one approaches such a witness, especially before an adversary attorney has entered the picture and advised that there is no obligation to speak, the more cooperative the witness is likely to be. One should always go to the session assuming the witness will talk, and be as fully prepared with documents and questions as possible.

Some attorneys are reluctant to conduct early interviews of possibly hostile witnesses, fearing that the interest thereby evidenced in the event will itself stir up claims and litigation. This view also suggests that facts should be held "close to the vest" when such interviews are conducted, to avoid disclosure to adversaries with the same effect. There is truth to these positions, but on balance I believe the benefits of the fullest possible early investigation outweigh the detriments. Insurance company claims departments have learned this through years of experience and thousands of cases, and try to get claims agents and investigators to the scene of an accident or hospital before the injured even knows whether there is a case. Knowledge of the controversy and the corporation's concern will get around soon enough anyway, and the pertinent facts will become known even if not disclosed in these interview sessions. Early interviews may well be the only way in which one can get access to the adversary's case and perceptions without the formality and limitations of judicial discovery. Moreover, one is hard put to conduct a sound interview if the inquiry is phrased too carefully and cutely, or the legitimate questions of the witness are parried.

As with so many company personnel, hostile witnesses have also learned something from the sporting approach. They frequently consider themselves amateur lawyers in its application. While they may be agreeable to speaking, they will rarely sign a statement or verify an affidavit. But they may be agreeable to examining the interviewer's notes, and either inking in a correction or suggesting that a change be made. In fact, handwritten notes of an interview showing a correction of the spelling of the witness's name or date of birth or address can be better evidence on cross-examination than a signed statement or verified affidavit. The witness may legitimately claim that the latter was drafted by the attorney and he or she didn't bother to read it carefully enough or correct it; that's hard to do when one has corrected the spelling of a name from two *t*'s to one. Some investigators, knowing this, deliberately make a mistake of this kind (such as by incorrectly recording a witness's date of birth), anticipating the change.

The same conduct to guard against with company documents and witnesses can also be used to aid in obtaining disclosures from hostile sources. Thus, even if ultimately one may not be able to discover an adversary's privileged communication, the judge will at least know its contents by virtue of a legitimate question as to whether such privilege in fact exists. Similarly, the kinds of persons who are important witnesses in socioscientific cases can be made to admit the bias or antagonism inherent in their conduct, even though they will rarely do so directly. They will, in fact, take the witness stand appearing as sweetness and light, genuinely believing that what they say is motivated solely by logic and reason. But at the same time they will have refused to take telephone calls or respond to letters, and will not voluntarily be interviewed. When questioned about this at a trial, the explanation may be lack of time, or avoidance of waste effort; but there's no such answer to their refusal to accept a certified or registered letter and sign the return receipt requested—especially if the mail has been left sealed, to be opened dramatically in the courtroom.

The "self-serving" document is a most useful tool with hostile witnesses in this category: the unanswered letter, requesting the opportunity of an interview at any time and place of the witness's choosing, with an offer to pay any reasonable incidental expense, including lost time; the record of telephone calls made and rejected; the return receipt marked by the Postal Service "Refused—Return to Sender"; the memorandum in an unmarked envelope, reciting the abortive circumstances of an interview, or unpleasant and hostile comments made, delivered by a third party and arguably constituting an "admission by silence." Sound litigation preparation requires that hostile witnesses be interviewed as much as friendly witnesses, or that some useful court evidence be available to explain the failure. The latter not only impeaches the credibility of the opposition, but enhances credibility of the corporation by demonstrating its determination to obtain and present the full story.

It probably need not be added in these post-Watergate days, but caution suggests a warning against the use of wiretaps or secret recordings of any kind, even where technically lawful. There still remains some question regarding the legal ethics involved, but the public antipathy and consequent risks to reputation are far too great to justify the comparatively minor advantage which might be gained. Privacy seems to be coming of age in America and should not lightly be interfered with.

Internal Management and Control

Total consistency in statement and conduct is fundamental to the rule-of-reason approach in socioscientific litigations. Modern filing methods and data-retrieval systems have already been noted as requisite to efficiency and economy; in the larger corporations, with numerous matters spanning the years in different jurisdictions, they are essential to substantive success. Cases may come and go, but the basic socioscientific issues have a way of continuing on and on. Often the same attorney will show up over and over on the other side, and government, labor, and even some of the larger consumer organizations are beginning to install their own advanced data recapture systems, which enable them to quote in one case what a different corporate executive said in another, or before a congressional committee, or in a public statement, or even in response to an environmental impact statement or other of the many documents available so freely under freedom-of-information acts. The struggle to develop the new rules governing our society is a never-ending one, and calls for a coordinated, integrated effort; it cannot be "played by ear." Winning it calls for use of the most efficient and modern techniques available.

Docket and Diary

Many professionals, including lawyers, consider themselves "thinkers and planners," and evidence little interest in the mechanics of organization. Yet mechanical control and tickler systems are needed to avoid error in scheduling and appointments, and to keep all the parts of an operation working smoothly together even when someone is sick, or has been transferred, or is working on a different emergency. In addition, by such measures the purely administrative aspects of the attorney's function are transferred to nonlegal personnel, who are not only better able to handle them but thereby give the attorney more time to work at his or her profession.

As in other matters requiring the installation of modern nonlegal equipment and techniques, the design of any specific docket system should be by experts, and should of course be geared to the corporation's other facilities and requirements. The function of the system remains the same however: to serve as a central litigation control, and as a reminder to the professionals of when something should be (or should have been) done. The simplest and most common example, and the one which sometimes causes attorneys who have overlooked or forgotten it to wake up at night in cold sweats, is the running of a statute of limitations. When a contract claim in favor of the corporation is received by the legal department, the last date on which suit can be commenced should be promptly entered into the docket system, and the attorney should thereafter be reminded at previously specified times (say six weeks, four weeks, three weeks, two weeks, and daily thereafter) in advance of the deadline. If the docket is not informed that the claim has been resolved or suit commenced at one of these points, it should be instructed to inform the attorney's immediate superior and thereafter others on up the line until some critical final time when no further delay can be accepted.

Conceptually it is best if the person in charge of the docket be an attorney, competent to review all matters received by the legal department and independently to make judgments as to what need be done. But such persons are hard to come by, and more commonly the docket manager will receive information from the attorneys involved, from legal department review procedures, and from forms prepared by the attorneys and outside counsel.

The value of a good docket/diary/tickler system becomes quickly apparent once it has been introduced, and many attorneys will use it to record other matters of which they should be reminded, such as documents needed for the annual meeting of stockholders, gatherings of professional associations, or even vacation schedules. A regular weekly or daily docket memorandum listing events by date and attorney involved can be circulated to the entire legal department and will serve as both a good general information sheet and as a management tool for the senior attorneys.

Filing

Whether litigation documents are processed centrally or by the individual staff attorney assigned, it is important that there be uniform and well-established filing procedures. Cases handled by different attorneys must be coordinated and litigations must be reviewed to determine important policy matters. Because emergencies are almost routine, attorneys may be unavailable when a key action has to be taken or a decision made. Others must be able to pick up and review the file quickly and efficiently, without having to search through what may sometimes be thousands of pages to find a pleading or draft of memorandum.

Small-claim files might be kept chronologically in one standard type of folder, with a brief description of the key concerns on the outside or facing cover. If the dispute progresses to the point at which court litigation ensues or outside counsel is retained, these files might be broken down to "pleadings," "memoranda," "correspondence," and "evidence." As they grow larger, the latter in turn might be broken down to "fact" and "law" memoranda, "internal" and "external" correspondence, "depositions," "exhibits," and other kinds of evidence and the like. Matters of different size can thereby be handled in accordance with their specific requirements, but with a uniform procedure known to all involved in litigation management.

It is desirable that a central facility be established through which incoming documents can be processed—i.e., stamped with the date and time of receipt and routed not only to the attorney assigned, but to others, including the docket manager, in accordance with specified procedures. It might be routine, for example, for the mailroom to send copies of all formal "pleadings" received to the docket manager, who in turn would enter the time for response or check off that an action called for had been taken, and to require notification of a substitute staff attorney whenever the primary attorney assigned is to be away for any extended period. Centralization will depend partly upon the volume of litigations administered, however, and it is essential only that there be some "regular course of business" way of routinely handling these ponderous and quite burdensome document matters.

Data Recapture

Physical and mechanical filing measures are of course the traditional way in which data is retrieved or recaptured. Modern, electronic data-processing systems, however, are more than just another way of doing the same thing more cheaply and effectively. They make it possible to present the affirmatives of corporate consistency and credibility in the socioscientific arena wherever and whenever appropriate, and not just by way of reactions to the challenges and attacks of adversaries.

Legal uncertainties as to course of action result largely from uncertainties regarding the facts. When these are removed or attenuated, the course becomes clear. And a clear course charted from the inception is the most credible of all. Given adequate time and manpower, even using antiquated methods, one can ordinarily help prepare the testimony of the corporation's chief executive for a deposition or hearing on some important environmental policy, for example, and be reasonably confident that nothing significant has been said or done to the contrary. With the assistance of the computer, however, the legal advocates speaking on behalf of the company can present that policy from the very beginning, even in informal discussions with regulatory authorities or consumer groups. They can examine it at each step as the matter progresses, and shape their approaches and actions accordingly. By the time the question has reached the dispute or litigation stage, most of the strategy will have been settled and the issue be only "what we've said all along."

Obviously one cannot introduce all corporate statements and actions into computer memory. But legislative testimony by key executives, important speeches and statements to stockholders, and significant public statements can certainly be entered. (Some corporations already record these for other purposes, such as public information.) Litigation documents and deposition and hearing testimony can be added as new cases proceed through investigation, discovery, and trial; important testimony and other evidence in older cases can be added as resources permit. Before long there will be a data bank of extremely useful information, pertinent to key concerns.

Review

Litigations are frequently processed much as any other corporate legal problem. They are assigned to a staff attorney for handling and are closely considered by others in the legal department only when the staff attorney requests assistance or something goes wrong. This may be acceptable for normal corporate problems, in which the staff attorney can become expert and where he or she is working with colleagues or friendly associates. But it is unacceptable practice in litigation, where by definition a hostile adversary is involved; where each matter is different and the procedural and substantive rules so varied all over the world that even the most experienced trial attorney must learn them in each case; where ordinarily the staff attorney is not a litigation specialist; where the vital task is to understand all others' perceptions of the issue, an assignment calling for as much help as one can get; and finally where the course of action chosen depends on the most sensitive judgments of the probable outcome of numerous different alternatives. The trial lawyer in a large law firm is able to call on the assistance and expertise of numerous partners and associates— the same should be true in the corporate legal department.

Corporate litigation review procedure should be standardized (although keyed to the needs of the particular case) and routinely applied to avoid suggesting criticism of any particular attorney.

The review group should include, as its head, the attorney in charge of litigations generally; as its secretary, the docket manager; and, as regular members, someone from the financial or insurance department concerned with evaluating exposure, and someone involved in investigations, preferably from the claims or investigating department if these functions exist. When his or her matters are under review, the assigned staff attorney should of course attend, plus other members of the litigation team as indicated by the anticipated nature of the discussion. If a particular area of substantive law is involved, the staff attorney expert in that specialty should participate. It is desirable, both to obtain additional perceptions and for general training purposes, that other staff attorneys also attend from time to time and participate in the discussions.

The review group should meet regularly, and in emergency session as required. Every dispute should be brought before it promptly following receipt so that a preliminary evaluation can be made and a tentative course of action approved.

Most matters will undoubtedly be relatively unimportant and the decisions obvious; where there are questions to be answered or further decisions to be made, however, the matter should be diaried forwarded to a subsequent meeting, with the appropriate docket entry mechanically entered. It should also be routine that matters will be automatically redocketed for review again at the end of standard periods of time, such as six months or one year, unless earlier review has been agreed upon or it has been concluded that the effort is not justified (as perhaps in the "stakeholder" or third-party title-clearing type of case, where there is little risk or exposure to the corporation). Action decided upon at the meeting, such as the filing of an application for administrative relief or the making of a motion, should be entered in the docket and followed up.

Because of the many details involved, it is desirable that forms be employed in the processing of litigation. The more significant forms, applicable at the stage when trial counsel has been retained, will be discussed in the next chapter. But the initiating form will be useful to the litigation review group and for control purposes at this early stage. Exhibit 2 is an example. It should be prepared by the assigned staff attorney or the docket manager. Most of its contents (apart from the purely descriptive entries) cannot be completed unless and until trial counsel is selected. Items 7 and 8

EXHIBIT 2 File Number:

LITIGATION REVIEW FORM

1. Title:
2. Description:
3. Court:
4. Nature of claim:
   — Monetary amount:
   — Other:
   — Insured?
5. Counsel
   — Firm:
   — Individual in charge:
   — Corporate attorney assigned:
6. Fee:
   — Written (attach copy to individual report)
   — Oral (describe arrangement):
7. Litigation plan:
   — Written (attach copy to initial report and as revised):
   — Oral (describe, including anticipated trial date):
8. Evaluation:
   — Maximum realistic exposure
      — Monetary:
      — Other:
   — Target result
      — Monetary:
      — Other:
   — Anticipated litigation costs:
9. Comment:
   — Does trial counsel advise currently?
   — Settlement appraisal?
   — Other?

---

and the possibility of settlement in Item 9, however, should be considered by the litigation review group at its first meeting, even though in many cases the tentative conclusions will be revised drastically thereafter.

Some comment may be appropriate regarding Item 4, a mechanical entry, and Item 8. Item 4 is the claim as stated by the adversary or client. Sometimes it will be realistic, but usually not. The common approach to litigations calls for a party to outline a claim in the most exaggerated way it thinks it can get away with. One of my colleagues once obtained a jury award in an amount higher than the *ad damnum* (demand) clause in his complaint, and was successful in persuading the appellate court on appeal that the jury had this right. The rather common reaction at the bar was not to praise him for having successfully won more than his client thought necessary to demand, but to condemn and criticize for having been so unwise as not to have exaggerated the claim to a figure higher than any jury could possibly have returned!

Item 8 calls for an evaluation of the "realistic" exposure incident to the case. This will be the staff attorney's best judgment of the outcome, as revised following discussions with the litigation group. It is an estimate of what will probably happen if the matter is handled properly from beginning to end, and includes the normal uncertainties and errors as well as good luck. It also calls for some judgment of the cost of carrying on the dispute, including the internal time of corporate legal and nonlegal personnel. If time and expense are not subject to control in this fashion, the estimate will have to be of the "ball park" variety, but this kind of information is as relevant to the evaluation of a matter as what one pays to or receives from an adversary.

Item 8 also calls for a "target" result. This is the hoped-for result—the best reasonable outcome one can anticipate, assuming the matter is handled in the best possible fashion throughout, with a maximum of good luck and a minimum of unavoidable error. It is the amount one would pay or accept at once to resolve the matter (perhaps sometimes plus or minus something to reflect litigation costs. This question will be considered in Chapter 5,

"Settlement"). It would obviously be critical for any independent financial evaluation purpose, although the amount of a reserve would more likely be based upon the "realistic" figure.

These figures are of course useful for corporate financial management and budget purposes, and are ordinarily developed in some manner when the fiscal-year-end audit takes place. But they are of special, independent utility to the corporate law department's litigation function. They distinguish the important cases, making it possible to focus attention on them. They serve as objective evidence of the progress of cases as evaluations are modified to reflect information developed during investigation, discovery, and pretrial. They constitute the staff attorney's authority to act. They let the staff attorney know that his or her ability will not be measured by whether "good" or "bad" cases are assigned, but based upon success in reaching the "target." As discussed later in Chapter 7, they help avoid the last-minute inadequate "courthouse step" settlement, motivated by a fear of going to trial. They make it possible for the managing attorneys, as well as appropriate other members of the litigating team, to participate in the important decisions. They concentrate the maximum of professional legal expertise on the real problem areas.

Cost Control

Item 8 of Exhibit 2 requires an ongoing evaluation of the costs of the litigation. Only a very preliminary guess is possible at the inception of a matter, but it is obviously a relevant concern. As the dispute proceeds, this figure can become literally gigantic. Outside legal fees and disbursements at the six-figure level annually are characteristic of the major socioscientific case; seven figures are not uncommon. Eight figures are not far around the corner. When internal costs of personnel time, including key executives, and travel, research, and other investigative expenses are added, the dimensions of the problem are apparent.

It may well be that a corporation will decide to adopt a given course of action as a matter of sound corporate policy, despite its expense. Defending certain kinds of unjustified antitrust claims may be judged necessary, for example, to avoid encouraging others to assert similar claims in an attempt to settle for something approaching the corporation's known large costs of litigation. But to proceed without analyzing cost can only be justified where the amounts are trivial. Proper cost analysis might have disclosed, for example, that the better course would be to withdraw from the business concerned, or to change policies, or to franchise the market out. Sound, relevant information is the cornerstone on which proper management and success are built.

Where the corporation's financial accounting methods permit, therefore, a separate account should be maintained for each litigated matter of significance. Personnel time, travel expenses, and all other direct costs should be charged to this account, together with some reasonable allocation of overhead. The information should be reported regularly and entered into the litigation review procedure. It should be compared with the anticipated figures, and judgments made as to the reasons for any discrepancies. The anticipated-cost figures should also be revised and updated as suggested by the experience.

Obtaining this kind of information should be relatively simple in most large corporations faced with rule-of-reason cases, with one surprising exception: Few law departments maintain the necessary records regarding attorney time. Lawyers seem constitutionally ill-equipped to change traditional ways. Even in the large corporation, which elsewhere employs advanced management information tools to control its inventory, finances, and operations generally, the legal department continues to function along old-fashioned lines. Attorneys are among the most expensive employees of a corporation and time is their sole resource, yet even the individual attorneys rarely know how they spend their days, and management is unable to accumulate the information for analytical purposes.

In any corporate legal department employing more than a minimum staff (that is, where the general counsel is not intimately privy to the details of all that is going on—perhaps five attorneys), each attorney should routinely record at least the time devoted to each separate litigation, on a daily basis. The figures should be accumulated weekly or monthly by attorney and matter, and thereafter by product, or department, or line of business, or type of claim, or geographical area, or otherwise as seems pertinent. The time, and related disbursements, should also of course be entered into the litigation account and review procedure so that all costs are reflected. Only in this way can management know its true litigation costs, and take action accordingly.

Where ten or more attorneys are involved, it will usually be cheaper to handle the information by computer methods. This can be processed in-house by the corporation's computer department, using computer software which is readily available on the open market. Independent computer data centers and time-sharing organizations also provide this same kind of service quite inexpensively.

If the attorney's total time is entered into the system, in addition to his or her litigation time, the procedure will also serve independently as a good law-department general-management tool. It will become quickly apparent, for example, that some areas of activity are requiring far more effort than they are worth, or that some attorneys need considerable guidance if they are to be efficient, or that the balance in assignments is out of line and transfers are needed. There is some danger here in that excessive and unreasonable time pressures can interfere with professionalism. Staff attorneys should not have to consider the value of every minute spent conferring with a colleague on a new Supreme Court decision, or justify every discussion with a corporate employee in terms of its dollar return. But properly utilized, the information will prove useful even to the individual attorneys themselves, some of whom will be astounded to learn how they spend their days.

Training and Education

Litigation is an after-acquired specialty, only a part of which can be learned in law school. By now it should be clear that I believe the staff attorney should work closely with trial counsel in the preparation and presentation of the rule-of-reason litigation. This process will have the incidental and important side effect of educating the staff attorney in the trial-law specialty, gradually enabling staff counsel (where he or she wishes) to assume more and more of the trial function, by conducting depositions, arguing motions, and even participating in and taking over trials. There is no sound reason, except the unavailability of trained manpower, for the large corporate law department not to be equipped to handle internally its regularly anticipated level of litigations, just as it handles other specialized legal functions. The resulting economies and efficiencies would be enormous. No outsider could possibly know corporate personnel and policy as intimately; no outsider could possibly be expected to speak so well for the client, especially under trying and difficult circumstances.

Even when the economics or requirements of a particular case do not justify it, for educational reasons staff attorneys should be encouraged to participate actively and intimately with trial counsel (younger attorneys in law firms are in this way educated), and the corporate attorney in charge of assigning litigations should include this training function in his or her decisions on the assignment of new matters.

The deliberations of the litigation group and other staff meetings can also be useful training tools. And where matters are expected to be of continuing general importance, video-cassette or tape presentations also will be effective. Should the corporation adopt the rule-of-reason approach for its litigations, for example, its general counsel might present it on video-cassette for viewing by all attorneys as they join the staff, as well as for presentation to outside retained trial counsel and even for use by company witnesses in their independent training programs.

Legal Research

Even though the facts in the socioscientific litigation usually require far more time and attention than the law, knowledge of the law is certainly essential. It is a rare corporate legal department that has the manpower needed to do the job adequately. The lengthy legal memorandum analyzing all aspects of a problem and citing all the cases from all the jurisdictions is ordinarily obtained from an outside law firm. (The desirability of accumulating all such legal memoranda and having them accessible rapidly will be treated in Chapter 4.) The corporate law department should consider using the many independent legal research services now available, some of which are quite good on problems where the issue can be stated simply and discretely. Computerized legal research is also being marketed in a growing number of jurisdictions. It is extremely efficient and makes possible certain kinds of inquiry which are not otherwise practical (for example, finding all the cases in which an adversary attorney has appeared in a certain court, or before a certain judge, or in connection with a particular type of matter). Not to be overlooked as an assist to research is the great value of identifying the substantive and procedural law specialists within the corporate legal department itself, and making clear their responsibility to advise and assist others with problems falling within their areas of expertise. Ordinarily there is no greater wealth of talent concerning the corporation's special legal problems than within the corporation itself. But too often responsibility is not adequately defined, and the specialist attorneys are so unavailable that those needing their help do the work themselves, assign it out or, unfortunately, too often don't do it at all.

Coordination

One of the most troublesome litigation problems is handling socioscientific issues that have global application. These are difficult cases, calling for substantial technical expertise and knowledge of the facts. Educating the many different legislative bodies, regulatory agencies, administrative and judicial tribunals, and others involved in the decision processes, including one's own corporate personnel and outside trial attorneys, can be a massive job. Moreover, much may be going on at the same time, so that the normal problem of maintaining consistency is necessarily magnified greatly.

Modern electronic devices are most useful. The video-cassette technique, already referred to, makes it possible to record factual descriptions or witness statements for training and education purposes, obviating the need for repetition every time a new problem arises. Statements and other documents can be transmitted quickly and cheaply by telecommunications. Word-processing equipment, a necessity in any organization with much paperwork, also permits the transmission of documents across great distances, with changes and corrections entered at different places and the complete job available in final form to all. Other techniques are appearing on the market all the time, and corporate experts in their employment should be consulted.

Obviously it is important that a single staff attorney be in charge of all the related matters, if necessary with others assisting. But sometimes, after court litigation has been commenced and outside trial counsel have been retained, it may be practically necessary to select someone as "lead" or "coordinating" counsel. Such a course calls for special attention by staff counsel.

Trial lawyers are a most competitive group: arguing, contesting and fighting in their day-in and day-out business. If they are good, they must be convinced of their own superiority in trial technique over all adversaries. Ask a successful trial lawyer who is the best litigator in the community and listen to (and watch) the response! In consequence, there is considerable friction inherent in the relationship when a client has selected one trial attorney to "lead" another. The follower is not accustomed to playing "second banana" to anyone but a client or superior within his or her own firm; nor to withholding comments and advice. Albeit subconsciously, the motivation to undercut and "show up" is inevitable, and the possibility of second guessing and "grandstand" or "Monday morning" quarterbacking (with appropriate apologies) is inherent in the situation. This prejudices the conduct of both leader and follower. Staff counsel can help minimize the problem by letting coordinating or lead counsel personally choose local counsel, or at least appear to let them do so. This places lead counsel more in the traditional role of client, and thus makes it easier for local trial lawyers to accept instructions and feel some measure of loyalty. On the other hand, corporate staff counsel must monitor matters regularly and make it clear to all that he or she continues to be their contact with the client. He or she should visit with local counsel and judiciously but still firmly obtain their judgments, to be sure they have not suppressed advice in the belief that lead counsel has already determined a course of action, or that lead counsel has not overruled them in uncertain areas without communicating the differences. Staff counsel should be sensitive to any friction that may be developing. To do all this without interfering with lead counsel's difficult assignment calls for all the personal talents staff counsel possesses.

The various measures outlined in this chapter are furnished only to provoke corporate counsel into giving thought to the tasks which must be carried out by the corporation seeking to adopt the rule-of-reason approach in its socioscientific litigations, and to suggest some of the almost unlimited kinds of administrative, mechanical, and electronic assistance available. Obviously the measures undertaken must vary from company to company, dependent upon financial and physical resources, the kinds of litigations anticipated, and even the personalities of corporate attorneys. As a result, specific adherence to a course of action as here proposed, or to a form as presented, is either strictly coincidental and fortuitous, or evidence that inadequate consideration has been given to the problem. Fortunately, the law is still a profession and calls for exercise of the most delicate and sensitive of judgments, after evaluating all the pertinent considerations. This book is intended as a resource only, not as a manual.

We turn now to the matter of selecting outside trial counsel—an activity usually considered to be the first step in corporate counsel's administration of a litigation but which, in the rule-of-reason case, is far on down the line.

Relations with Trial Counsel

Chapter **4**

Retention of trial counsel is one of corporate counsel's most important litigation functions. It is discussed at this relatively late point only to emphasize that the final outcome of litigation is for the most part predetermined long before trial counsel enters the picture.

Corporate counsel's retention of new outside counsel to handle a major socioscientific litigation commonly proceeds as follows: Confidential and discreet inquiry will be made among business and legal colleagues and friends, seeking to identify the most competent trial lawyer in the area concerned, preferably in a large and prestigious firm. When a prime candidate has been selected, an introduction is arranged and a preliminary approach made to determine whether the firm is interested, whether it has any conflicts, and whether it is otherwise in a position to handle the matter. If this step is affirmative, a personal meeting takes place, usually in the trial attorney's office, attended by corporate counsel and the trial attorney and those of the latter's partners and associates whom he or she believes should be involved in the retainer discussions.

Following the amenities, trial counsel will state that he or she has looked at the papers furnished and has studied the matter with colleagues, of course only in the most preliminary way. They like the case, have recently had experience which is similar and will be helpful, believe they can do a fine job for the client, and would welcome the opportunity to enter into what they regard as a most challenging as well as pleasant professional and personal relationship. Of course there can be no assurances or guarantees of success, but they promise the best and most effective possible representation, and hope the client will be so well satisfied at the conclusion that a mutually attractive, long-term relationship will result.

Corporate counsel's purpose in arranging the face-to-face meeting is really only to see whether superficial appearances or the personalities involved would render the representation inappropriate. After all, background and reputation have already been checked, and the time to answer or to take other procedural action is fast running out. In addition, how much can one really tell from a necessarily brief and cursory session? If nothing seems untoward, agreement on representation is therefore quickly reached and the discussion turns to fee.

Trial counsel, or another partner who has introduced the matter to the firm, will point out that there is no way at this early stage to predict the course of the litigation with any reasonable degree of accuracy. Conceivably it may be resolved by settlement or preliminary motion at a very early point; but just as conceivably it will go on for years, with lengthy depositions and investigations, examination of thousands or millions of documents, motions, hearings, even appeals. Certainly it is a "big" case and the firm's experience is that the only fair way to handle fees in such matters is on the basis of time. The firm knows the stature and reputation of the client, so no advance dollar retainer will be requested. It will of course listen to any other proposal, but quite frankly is confident nothing else will work out as equitably for all concerned. The firm will do its best whatever the fee, and sees no reason why it should receive a bonus simply because the result turns out good; similarly, it would be unfair of the client to penalize the firm if, despite all proper efforts, the case is a bad one and is lost. The firm's overhead is so substantial that it is most reluctant to enter into contingent-fee arrangements, and this is not a situation where a contingent-fee relationship is essential because the client lacks the funds necessary to its representation. In any event, corporate counsel as an attorney surely knows that contingent fees in the long run usually cost the client more than payment on the equivalent of a "time and materials" basis.

All of this is reasonable enough and the matter may end there. But sometimes an aggressive corporate counsel will ask about hourly rates—what are they and how are they handled? Very frequently the response will be that the firm considers this information confidential. However, it can assure the client that its rates are for all practical purposes the same as those of other similar firms in the area; the real difference in charges is obviously in how much work the attorney concerned turns out in any given period of time, and of what quality. The firm may, with or without pressure, go further and report that its rates range from a minimum (say $40 per hour) for the youngest attorney fresh out of law school, to a maximum (say $175 per hour) for the senior partner, and that past studies of the "mix" in cases such as the one concerned indicate an average of about $72 per hour. This average can be lowered quite substantially through the use of the firm's paralegals (for whom the charge will be $25 per hour), and more recent random surveys suggest that the firm is getting its average hourly rates in matters of this kind down to approximately $60 per hour. Furthermore, although the firm may only bill for its professional services from time to time (sometimes even annually), it will submit disbursement bills monthly and will be glad to report its accumulated time charges at the same time. This will give the client a good "handle" on what is going on without disclosing confidential data.

If corporate counsel continues to press, the firm may also make reference to its computerized time controls, which require every attorney to submit a daily report of the time spent on each matter for each client. It will say that these are accumulated and analyzed by the partner in charge of each client and each matter to be sure that time is being employed effectively and efficiently. If time appears to have been wasted, or an attorney is particularly slow, or an effort turns out to have been one somehow useful for training purposes only, the time will be charged to one of the numerous firm overhead accounts and not billed to the client at all. The firm prides itself on its own internal management controls and regards its own reputation at stake in these matters.

It is a very rare corporate counsel indeed who will push further for regular reports of work done, by attorney, paralegal, time, dollar rate, and other internal firm breakdown. Instead, long before this time the conversation will have turned to keeping the "average" hourly rate at the lowest reasonable level. It requires no mathematician to recognize that the 1,000 hours of monthly work estimated as required during at least the initial investigative stages of the litigation is $175,000 per month for the most senior partner and only $40,000 per month for the young associate; if paralegal help alone is used, it would decrease to $25,000 per month. Multiplied by twelve, to accord with the corporate legal department's annual budget, the difference is enormous. It may spell the difference between routine internal law-department administration and regular executive committee or board of directors reports and review. Accordingly, corporate counsel will sometimes almost insist that work within the firm be handled at the lowest professional level consistent with the quality required. The firm will not only give such assurances, but reply that it is firm policy. Of course, the trial partner will maintain supervision to insure uniformly high quality, but once the litigation strategy has been developed and the case is under way his or her time involvement will remain minimal until the major depositions are taken and final preparation for trial begins. Furthermore, special emphasis will be placed on using paralegal help where possible, especially in indexing and controlling the massive numbers of documents anticipated.

Finally the discussion will turn to litigation strategy. The firm will point out that its analysis of the facts and law has obviously been most limited, but that it appears superficially that substantial discovery will be taken on both sides, and that a number of procedural motions and other applications will be in order. It wants to begin promptly investigating the facts and will send a team of attorneys and paralegals to the client's main offices to begin assembling documents and interviewing witnesses. It considers that priority of discovery is important and will serve notices of depositions with its answer. Later it will also serve document requests, but right now it wants to "freeze" the stories of the opposition before they learn too much of the corporation's case. There is no way of predicting precisely when the trial will take place, but the calendar of the local court is much delayed and in all likelihood the case will not come to trial for three or four years.

By now the hour is late and counsel is anxious not to miss the last plane home. The strategy sounds good and corporate counsel's response probably will be to tell the trial firm to use its judgment and proceed aggressively. Reports from time to time would be appreciated, certainly of major developments, but he or she is not a trial lawyer and does not want to try to "second guess" trial counsel. The firm is being retained because of its trial expertise and corporate counsel not only wants to rely on that expertise but is almost as busy as they are. Staff counsel will be glad to help wherever they can, particularly in arranging contacts with fellow corporate executives and others in the company, but otherwise would prefer just being kept up to date and generally informed. The firm may reply that it prides itself on its ability to do just this, and itself prefers that kind of a relationship.

The above may be acceptable to the traditional litigation approach, although I believe that even there it is unwise in view of the major differences between the perceptions of outside trial counsel and their corporate clients, and the omnipresent possibility of inadequacy or error. But in rule-of-reason litigation it is almost Kafkaesque. Recall Joseph K in Kafka's *The Trial*, who at the end is led away meekly to be executed by strangers he has never seen before, carrying out a sentence of which he has not been told, rendered by judges before whom he could not appear, based on evidence of which he was not informed, for a crime about which no one would advise him. Here the corporation has gone to outside counsel for expertise and then demanded that the expert so carefully chosen spend the least possible time and assign the youngest and least expert members of the staff to its case. It has agreed to pay hundreds of thousands or millions of dollars for time to be spent, but is not to be told who is spending the time, when and for what. Even the firm's assurance that the rates are "competitive" suggests that the information is kept in greater confidence from the client than from the firm's competitors. Most important, the corporation is retaining others to speak for it and represent its total position to the community and the world—without being certain they understand general corporate policy and other essential aspects of that position, and without knowing in advance what they will do or say. The corporation has abdicated its essential full responsibility and control over who does and who does not do what on its behalf.

Rule-of-reason litigation demands that trial counsel be an extension of the corporation's presence, and almost as much a part of the corporation as any department or executive or official. Indeed, corporations adopting the rule-of-reason approach will undoubtedly gradually build up their own internal staffs of competent trial lawyers, intimately informed as to the corporation's policies and business; a very few corporations already have. But until that happens, the tightest possible relationship with outside counsel is essential both for success and economic effectiveness. In the typical retainer arrangement the exact opposite is the case.

As professionals, trial counsel may resist interference with what they regard as their own legitimate areas of expertise— examination and cross-examination, how to open and sum up to a jury, how most effectively to present an argument to an appellate court. But even in these areas, they should not resist constructive suggestion and assistance if the need is adequately explained. And in other significant matters involving corporate credibility, they will appreciate that they are advocates, not principals. Most will be quick to acknowledge that their roles require presentation only of those positions a client determines to be in its best interest. This justifies intimate client participation in the litigation process, and supervision and direction where appropriate. Any trial attorney who seeks to interpose his or her own commercial judgment for that of a client is overstepping proper bounds.

Maintaining the necessary close relationship between corporate and trial counsel is not only possible, therefore, but can be carried out in the most professional fashion. It requires, however, that the guidelines be laid out clearly from the inception, so that trial counsel will not view a change in approach as criticism or dissatisfaction. It must also be made clear that this approach is standard corporate policy, not the result of doubt or suspicion about the ability of this particular trial counsel. Printed procedures or forms (which are especially useful to younger and less experienced corporate staff counsel, understandably reluctant to insist on their own views with outside expert seniors), or at least carefully stated introductory phrases ("This is corporate policy") will be effective in conveying this idea. The balance of this chapter is devoted to specific suggestions in these connections.

Selection of Trial Counsel

Trial lawyers are an independent lot and some will insist on doing things their own way irrespective of instructions—they are convinced they know what is best. Such attorneys are few, but they do exist. Obviously they cannot be permitted to handle rule-of-reason litigations.

With that exception, however, I know of no difference between the qualifications required of trial counsel in the ordinary and in the rule-of-reason case. One selects counsel in the same fashion one selects the heart surgeon—on the basis of qualifications. How many cases has he or she tried? What kind? What is his or her reputation? What professional honors or achievements has counsel earned? What do this attorney's briefs, depositions, and trial transcripts look like? What kind of a firm is he or she with? Does it have the manpower to handle the matter? What is its reputation?

These questions could go on and on. They obviously will be geared to the particular case and situation and need no elucidation here. But the significance of actual live court experience deserves emphasis because it is so often overlooked. People are often called trial lawyers who are not, especially in the larger firms. They may well have been involved in motion practice, depositions, and even appeals; but most cases are settled before trial, and actual court experience in the large firm is much more uncommon than is generally understood. "Big" cases represent enormous risks to law firms, as they do to clients, and attorneys without actual court experience are only gradually and reluctantly permitted to handle them in court. The result is a kind of self-perpetuating status—the attorney without actual court experience is prevented from acquiring actual court experience because he or she hasn't had it. It is partly for this reason that so many ambitious attorneys leave the big firms to join a district attorney's or other government litigation office, and thereby gain the experience denied them in the firm.

Where the information has not been developed in the initial check, therefore, inquiry should always be made regarding the specific number and kinds of cases which have been personally handled during trial by the trial attorney recommended. Where there is doubt, one might review one or more trial transcripts to see who opened and summed up, who asked the questions of the important witnesses, and who made the objections.

Some other general comments applicable to the selection of trial counsel for a major socioscientific litigation:

1. *Select the lawyer, not the firm.* Lawyers are professionals, and even the largest institutionalized firms are relatively loose agglomerations of people. Quality varies, and it does no good to have the finest firm if the individual attorney assigned is less than the best. Emphasis should be on selecting the trial attorney first, and then his or her firm. And it should be made clear from the inception that the attorney selected will continue in charge, from beginning to end.

2. *Prefer the trial specialist.* Modern socioscientific cases usually involve specialized substantive law and complex scientific issues, including patent or tax law, or nuclear physics or biochemistry. Where possible, one should of course seek to retain a trial lawyer with background in all the appropriate specialties. But normally this is impossible. Where a choice must be made, the trial specialist should be preferred—choose the trial lawyer without patent experience to try the patent litigation rather than the patent lawyer without trial experience. Trial law is a specialty every bit as much as any other—more so in one respect, because, unlike other specialties, there is often so little time to study and reflect

before having to act. The trial lawyer cannot render a patent opinion that calls for the broad, general knowledge of the specialist to make possible the discovery of problems and the suggestion of solutions. But he or she can learn the relatively limited amount of patent law needed for a litigation. Trial counsel is trained to move from one problem area to another; rarely are two cases the same. However complex a litigation may be, the issues will be defined and the problems narrowed to discrete and limited ones by the adversary process itself. One can often know the conclusion to be fought for, without knowing any of the analysis to be supplied later. But the patent lawyer cannot litigate without years of trial experience, any more than the trial lawyer can render a sound patent opinion.

3. *Choose local over remote counsel.* Rule-of-reason litigations in particular are decided on the basis of attitudes, prejudices, and emotions. These vary from locality to locality all over the United States, and it is best wherever possible to retain local trial counsel who is personally well advised in these respects. Moreover, even where out-of-town trial counsel is retained, local court rules almost always require that local counsel be employed as well. One cook is better than two, especially when dealing with personalities as aggressive and unique as those of trial attorneys.

4. *Do not fear to retain a smaller firm.* All too frequently corporate counsel automatically selects the largest firm in the community without adequately considering those down the line. Perhaps this is the result of a normal concern at being "second-guessed" by top management if something later goes wrong. After all, if one has selected the biggest and most successful firm in the area one cannot be faulted seriously; selecting a smaller firm "on the come" can more easily turn out to have been a mistake.

Law firms, however, seem to have cycles similar to business cycles; very often when they are at their peak, they are also just beginning the way down. Consider the number which have brought in the fresh, prestigious blood of governors, senators, or judges to bolster their reputations or attractiveness. The reasons for the cycles are many and varied, but most important undoubtedly is that the best young law-school graduates will go where there is opportunity for rapid advancement, and sometimes see the chances for partnership and success at the largest firms as less attractive than those at the next size level. Do not hesitate, therefore, to consider the medium-size firm which is expanding, and which others in the area may even mildly reproach for aggressiveness. It must be large enough, of course, to handle a matter which on occasion may call for the services of a substantial number of partners and associates, but it need not necessarily be the giant of the community.

5. *Combine credit with responsibility.* One final general comment regarding internal firm politics. All large firms have the problem of allocating profits. In one fashion or another these allocations are predicated upon client-getting or client-retaining abilities, and upon work output. Often these two abilities are joined—the partner who brings in the client will also be in direct and immediate charge of the work. But not infrequently the two are divorced. The client should not permit this to happen, and should try to insure that the trial lawyer handling the litigation will also be the "credit" partner. Billings show that it is not uncommon for the "credit" partner, who is concerned most intimately with continued client representation, generally to charge a different percentage of standard rates than the "working" partner, whose most intimate concern is production in the specific matter. The power of the partner to insist upon assignment of the best personnel and to gain other priorities is also restricted when the two roles are separated; in other respects the client and litigation suffer when the functions are apart. It may be difficult for corporate counsel, especially in light of a long relationship with the aged senior partner, to do so, but he or she should manage the initial discussions so that the trial partner assigned to be in charge of the litigation will also be

given credit for billing as well as for work done. Simply identifying that attorney as the reason for the retainer should in most cases ensure this.

The Retainer Agreement

Once senior trial counsel has been selected, the function of corporate counsel in negotiating the details of the retainer agreement is to develop an understanding that will serve the overall purpose of insuring the highest possible quality of legal effort at the lowest reasonable cost. Perhaps surprisingly to some, almost the least significant consideration is the hourly dollar rate per attorney. Such figures *are* relatively standard within the same kinds of firms in any community, and $125 or $150 per hour is no more ridiculous to pay for the true expertise of a trial lawyer than several multiples of that amount for the sensitive hands of a heart surgeon. Indeed, the five-minute antitrust specialist's summary of cases and authorities studied over the years can save another attorney dozens of research hours or more and thereby have a value not related to time at all. But $25 or $40 per hour *is* ridiculous to pay for work which is essentially that of a file clerk, or work which is unneeded or duplicative, or work which could be accomplished much more effectively within the corporation as part of a long-range training program designed to remedy the problems that led to the litigation in the first place.

The retainer negotiation should establish corporate counsel's necessary degree of participation in litigation strategy and tactics, and permit him or her a continuing role in managing the quality of the assignments and work and in seeing that time is spent efficiently. The differences between attorneys (and in working *relationships* between junior and senior attorneys) are tremendous. One attorney may be able to turn out a polished affidavit or brief in just a few hours, requiring only the most cursory review; a second may take days for the same job, and even then come up with a product that requires as much writing and rewriting by the partner in charge as if there had been no preliminary draft at all.

Far better to see that young associates don't waste hours writing and correcting unacceptable, inadequate, or unnecessary memoranda than try to shave a rate from $40 to $38 per hour.

One other preliminary comment: It would be most unfortunate if the need to participate intimately in litigation management were somehow permitted to interfere with what should be the highest form of professional relationship. Corporate counsel should take particular care to explain that these measures are requested only because he or she wishes to work closely with trial counsel in the representation of the client, and that they do not in any way reflect doubts or suspicions about the quality or integrity of the litigation specialist. Corporate counsel wishes to discuss and suggest, but in final analysis intends fully to rely on the retained trial attorney in matters involving litigation expertise. If the management methods recommended here are permitted to result in fencing, antagonism, or bitterness, the professional relationship will be impaired and the litigation will inevitably suffer.

The Litigation Plan

The most significant aspect of the trial attorney's assignment is frequently the one least discussed—his or her plan for achieving the client's objective.

Good trial lawyers are very busy and in great demand, and quite often move rapidly from one case to the next. As a result, sometimes the need continually to revise and update litigation strategy is overlooked. Sometimes indeed there is no plan at all, other than what is dictated by the court rules and procedures or the actions of an adversary requiring response. The trial strategy may have been outlined in a limited and preliminary way during the retainer discussion ("We'll need a good bit of discovery, but should be able to make a motion for summary judgment"), but what happens thereafter bears little resemblance to it.

Good trial practice requires that the trial lawyer be as much in command of the case as possible, not simply responsive to the demands of court calendar or adversary activity. Even if only in the most preliminary fashion, he or she usually will have outlined a plan of action during the retainer discussion. Corporate counsel should hold trial counsel to that plan, as it may be expanded and updated from time to time thereafter; there is no excuse for permitting the product furnished to turn out other than in accordance with specifications.

One way to accomplish this is to request trial counsel at the retainer discussion to prepare, or participate in the preparation of, a formal "litigation preparation plan." Exhibit 3 exemplifies such a form, which might be printed and taken to the initial meeting to underscore that this is routine corporate policy. Obviously the form can be filled out only in the broadest and most general fashion at the inception of the case, but there will always be *some* initial factual investigation and pleadings, there will usually be some consideration given to possible motions, discovery, and settlement, and there will be at least a guess as to the trial date. The form does not ask for assurances or guarantees; it does ask for one's present estimate as to a trial date, for example, and that corporate counsel be informed as that estimate changes.

The litigation preparation plan serves a number of extremely useful functions. First, it represents the authority given to trial counsel. Except in the case of extreme emergency, it would be difficult to justify his or her making a motion of any significance, such as to dismiss or for summary judgment, unless the plan contains reference to such a motion. Trial counsel ordinarily should not even undertake the research required for the effort in the absence of a prior indication that the possibility of the motion was under consideration.

Second, the plan requires that the extremely valuable careful attention given to planning and strategy at the inception be carried on throughout; this kind of effort is the very essence of the great trial law firm's expertise, and is too often not repeated thereafter. Use of the plan means that the case will not get lost in the shuffle of the law firm. The young attorneys carrying the burden of the work while the trial partner is engaged in another lengthy trial cannot simply take over, as too frequently happens.

EXHIBIT 3

LITIGATION PREPARATION PLAN

(To be revised as appropriate, and kept current)

Anticipated timetable
for commencement
and/or completion

I. Initial factual investigation
II. Pleadings
III. Motions (specify)
IV. Affirmative discovery
   1. oral depositions
   2. documents
   3. interrogatories
   4. admissions
   5. other (describe)
V. Disclosure to adversary
   1. preparation of deponents
   2. documents
   3. interrogatories
   4. other (describe)
VI. Settlement
VII. Trial
   1. trial fact and law memos
   2. witness preparation
   3. preparation of cross-examination

Third, the formal plan promises corporate counsel the necessary opportunity to participate in strategy. He or she should surely inquire, for example, about the purpose and significance of any strategy changes that seem questionable. Trial lawyers often assume that their reasons for a course of action are so esoteric or require so much trial experience that an outsider couldn't possibly understand. The corporate attorney cannot accept this—there *must* be an explanation. He or she should insist upon understanding it, even if this requires a display of ignorance in the matter.

Fourth, the formal litigation plan serves as a control in those few but unavoidable cases where something goes wrong. If its contents are incorporated into corporate counsel's docket and diary system, discussed in Chapter 3, it will become immediately apparent that witnesses haven't been seen as scheduled, that documents haven't been collected, that depositions haven't been taken. There will be no last-minute calls on the eve of trial requiring that a disastrous settlement be accepted because "we're not ready."

And fifth, the plan serves as a part of the overall litigation control mechanism. The latter furnishes corporate counsel an opportunity to evaluate the efficacy of assistants working on the case; makes possible access to the firm's work product of law and fact research for use in other cases and situations; and adds the corporation's perceptions to those of the trial attorney in the management of the litigation. How this works requires an explanation of the regular reporting mechanism, to be discussed next.

Report of Pending Litigation

Exhibit 4 represents the "report of pending litigation," which might also be a printed corporate form brought to the retainer conference. Note that the penultimate item calls for a report as to whether there have been any changes in the litigation preparation plan and, if so, attachment of a copy of the revision. When this form is used, there can be no excuse for an outdated plan. Nor can the trial attorney or colleagues properly claim to have overlooked it.

In one form or other, the information contained in the litigation report is used for billing and management purposes in any well-managed law firm. It has equal or greater utility to the corporate client. Regular analysis of the report, and introduction of the information and documents obtained into corporate counsel's

EXHIBIT 4
REPORT OF PENDING LITIGATION
(To be furnished monthly or when charges exceed
$2,500, whichever comes *last*)

I. Professional charges:

Name	Hours	Rate	Total
1.			
2.			
3.			
4.			

II. Professional services:

1. Pleadings   attach copies if not previously furnished
2. Motions   "   "   " "   "   "
3. Memos of fact   "   "   " "   "   "
4. Memos of law   "   "   " "   "   "
5. Other   describe

III. Disbursements:

1. Transportation
2. Hotel
3. Meals
4. Long distance telephone
5. Duplicating
6. Overtime
7. Outside services
   a. investigations
   b. transcripts and reporting
   c. other (describe)
8. Other (describe)

IV. Revision of litigation preparation plan?   Yes——— No———
(If revised, attach copy.)

V. Brief status report.

docket and information retrieval systems (also discussed in the preceding chapter), will produce reams of information.

The first item, professional charges, is *not* included as a check on the law firm's reporting of hours and extrapolation of dollars. Even the smaller law firms today use EDP methods of recording these figures, and any errors of significance would certainly turn up through other checks without the need for this kind of elaborate reporting. Instead, this category of information is designed to determine who is working on the case and obtain some measure of their efficiency. The quality of lawyers varies. When one obtains regular reports of the time spent by Jones, Smith, Brown, and Green, and examines their product (Exhibit 4, Item II), one can tell quite quickly who is fast and who is slow; who is perceptive and who is not; who is putting in longer hours (perhaps because of criticism for not working hard enough) and who is putting in shorter (perhaps because of the opposite); who is drafting and revising to impress the senior partners rather than in the interest of the client; who has been transferred or "rotated" away from the matter, despite a tremendous investment in his or her education in the case; who has been rotated in and is doing work which requires background information, and which would be much more efficiently handled by another; whether a project seems to have been chosen more to protect the firm's reputation than to benefit the litigation; whether there are differences in the discretionary reporting of time. (In regard to this last point, some attorneys, for example, treat the time spent keeping up to date in their general substantive specialty, such as by reading advance sheets, as˜chargeable if they are working full time in that specialty for a client; others do not. There are many such possible variations, some of which will be discussed later in this chapter.) The permutations and combinations of management information gleaned are almost unlimited; frequently the law firm itself may not have undertaken the full analysis and will find corporate counsel's suggestions challenging and constructive.

All these items will of course require detailed discussion during the retainer conference. It may do little good to learn that an associate who has been trained in the client's business is being "rotated" if one has not previously established that those assigned to the parts of the case requiring lengthy training and background will stay with it until its conclusion. Similarly, it is impossible to complain effectively about the inexperience of persons assigned to one's litigation if, at the inception, one has solicited agreement to use the least-experienced personnel whenever possible.

It is my belief that during retainer discussions corporate counsel should make clear that he or she is hoping to use trial counsel as the corporation's litigating resource because the corporation lacks some essential litigation expertise. As much as possible, corporate counsel should handle in-house any work not calling for such expertise, including actual pretrial and trial presentations. Ordinarily there is no reason why indexing and controlling documents, for example, cannot be handled internally or by one of the outside service bureaus now specializing in these kinds of matters —in both cases, of course, under the general supervision of trial counsel. One needs the heart surgeon to operate and prescribe; one does not need the surgeon to administer aspirin in accordance with prescription or to take temperature hourly to see whether it exceeds 100°.

Similarly, in large litigations, the use of paralegals and young law associates very often represents a major part of the expense, running into the six-figure level a month. I believe that corporate counsel can and should do much of the internal factual investigation and preparation and even legal research. (In both these areas, as discussed in Chapter 3, quite competent outside organizations are also available, including computerized legal research sources, at small fractions of the cost of trial counsel.) Again, trial counsel should supervise, but corporate counsel's legal staff should be just as competent to perform legal research or undertake factual investigations as the law-firm associate fresh out of law school— if not, corporate counsel should improve his or her staff. And the corporate employee reading, digesting, and indexing documents should be as competent to do so as the law-firm paralegal, hired without training.

Corporate counsel should also seek during the retainer conference, or as soon thereafter as possible, to meet all the attorneys to be assigned to the litigation and to exercise at least some influence in their selection. Qualified, experienced associates *are* hard to come by, but they do exist and should be sought. Corporate counsel should try to obtain the assignment of attorneys who have satisfactorily worked on an earlier matter for the corporation and therefore have some knowledge of its business and personnel. As suggested earlier, he or she should request assurances that those assigned to areas requiring special training and education in the applicable facts or law will remain with the case until its conclusion. The amount of time wasted by both sides (corporation as well as law firm) in just meeting new people, getting acquainted, learning the special language, and finding out what goes where, can be enormous, and represents an important area of potential cost reduction.

Law firms quite properly have training programs, and outside interference with them should and will meet resistance. But if these matters are considered at the inception of relations they will ordinarily present no problems. If the firm understands that the client wants the attorney assigned to stay with the matter throughout, it will select an individual who is a long way from rotation, or who has requested an assignment of this kind, or who for some other reason can be expected to fit the necessary commitment into his or her long-range schedule. Corporate counsel can help by letting both the junior attorney and the firm know how satisfied the client is and by indicating to the attorney that the client will contribute positively to his or her future with the firm. Few young attorneys in the larger law firms can lay claim to some significant relationship to a large client's business. The carrot, properly held out, represents a substantial inducement.

One other aspect deserves discussion at this point. For some reason, even the toughest and most aggressive corporate counsel seem to feel they must be "good guys" in dealing with their outside law firms. Corporate counsel may have requested, for example, a rush memorandum outlining the current status of discovery to present to the board of directors. The senior associate assigned to the case will be working on it when suddenly the partner in charge (in a hundred-person law firm) will telephone and say that an emergency litigation has just been called for trial, and the associate is desperately needed to help. Would the client mind if the memorandum is postponed to the next board meeting? Surely the client minds; but clearly the trial emergency is more urgent than the board report and permission is given with a request that the memorandum be completed as promptly as possible after the trial.

Why didn't corporate counsel ask, "Why me?" Has the partner gone through every other assignment in the firm and made a judgment that this is the least significant? Isn't it more likely that the partner hasn't been able to convince any other partners to give up any of their senior, much-sought-after associates, or hasn't even tried, and has chosen this one because the client is a "good guy" and is expected not to complain? Or perhaps it may be that the partner or firm was just too ambitious and accepted a new client or new matter that they weren't in a position to handle. At the least, corporate counsel might have sought assurances that the other alternatives didn't exist and obtained positive indication that the firm would not in the future accept new matters it wasn't able to handle. One or two episodes of that kind and such demands won't reoccur. The squeaky wheel does get the oil, even in law practice. One can be nice without being a "sucker." And the fact also is that outside law firms respect the corporate counsel who knows what he or she is doing and accepts no foolishness. The law is a profession and should be treated as one—but it is also a business. There is some necessary adversary element in the relationship of attorney and client (is there anything more adversarial than negotiating a fee?) and no reason why the insistence upon recognition of one's rights in an area of conflict is any less ethical or professional than such insistence in the traditional adversary litigation context.

Obtaining the Litigation File

Item II of the litigation report form calls for a report of the professional services rendered during the period. The trial attorney is also to furnish physical copies of the documents involved, not merely a verbal description.

I believe that corporate counsel should have a substantial duplicate of trial counsel's file, down to drafts of briefs and memos and correspondence with court, adversary, and witnesses, furnished in a timely fashion. Such information is of course useful in evaluating the nature of the services rendered and in making suggestions for improvement, but that is by no means its sole or even its most important purpose.

A routine review of all litigation documents as prepared is one of the most effective ways in which corporate counsel can participate in trial counsel's deliberations. If one can see the draft of a motion and supporting papers, one can add facts and· arguments, make suggestions as to approach, and evaluate risks. In rule-of-reason litigation, where the entire corporate presence is involved, the opportunity is invaluable.

Ongoing participation in the document development stages also permits corporate counsel to insert his or her own perception of what should and what should not be done, and by whom. A memorandum of law, for example, might better be done in-house —it might even have just been completed by other trial counsel in connection with another case in another jurisdiction. Or the corporation might conclude that the obvious costs of the research are much too great in view of the minor benefit sought, or that in any event, the point of law is not one it chooses to assert as a matter of corporate policy, irrespective of how the research turns out. There is huge waste in legal and factual research into areas which should never have been covered, or which might have been developed far better in some other fashion.

Similarly, the introduction of such memoranda into the corporation's retrieval system makes it possible to access them for other cases at other times. Law firms generally index and file their memoranda for future reference; why shouldn't the client who pays for them? Does it make sense for law firms working independently for the same client in different parts of the country to each research independently the federal law of *forum non conveniens?* (Incidentally, this kind of thing also keeps firms on their toes. Lawyers are a competitive lot—even if they do share some cost information—and the knowledge that a competitor somewhere may try to poke holes in their work can have a salutary effect. In addition, the knowledge that their costs may be compared can also be beneficial.)

There may initially be some reluctance to furnish these kinds of documents, especially drafts, on the grounds that they are the law firm's "work product." They may in fact be work product, but that is only a conditional exemption from production to an adversary, not to the client. The firm may also protest that drafts should not leave the premises, because they do not represent a final considered product and might be misunderstood. The answer is to mark them boldly as such (not to subject them to the full and expensive panoply of partnership review and opinion giving), and to assure the firm they will be made available only to other attorneys for the client, who will appreciate their preliminary or tentative nature. (The final suggestion, that these documents represent leverage in the event of change of trial counsel and fee dispute, will not ordinarily be stated. But some of this occurs, and it is just as well for corporate counsel not to be without recourse of their own. Indeed, for this same reason, corporate counsel should where possible avoid escrow agreements and other relationships that involve a commitment to a single named trial counsel.)

Another significant purpose in document review is to stimulate the law firm's own internal evaluation of the quality of its professional output and the validity of its time charges. All firms have procedures designed to evaluate the work of their attorneys, and even those most dedicated to hourly charges will delete time spent improperly. But these are objectives to be sought and do not always work out as planned any more than do the internal management controls of a corporation. The reviewing partner gets sick, or takes a vacation, or goes into an extended trial, or may have other internal firm problems. When the regular litigation report requires this kind of detail, however, someone is much more likely to look at the time spent and the related work done to see if anything is out of line. If an attorney has spent 155 hours and produced only a memorandum of law discussing the applicable statute of limitations, an explanation will be sought or corrective action taken, including reduction of the time billed. The knowledge that the client can and will conduct a check is therefore of substantial independent importance.

The process of keeping corporate counsel informed of developments is also useful to trial counsel as later justification of charges for professional services. All too often trial lawyers undertake an assignment and proceed substantially alone through investigation, motions, depositions, document discovery, prehearing conferences, and other pretrial proceedings, without ever informing the client of what is going on. Then, when settlement comes, they cannot understand why the client objects so strenuously to the bill presented, failing to appreciate that the client cannot evaluate the extent of their services unless informed of what they are doing. Wholly apart from the important substantive benefits of client participation, as a matter of sound business and financial practice trial attorneys should keep the client informed of what is being done on an intimate and continuing basis.

Time and Disbursement Policies

The computer is an intimidating device. It is amazing how almost without exception corporate counsel accept its output of hourly times, rates, and charges, without ever inquiring as to the content of computer input. In socioscientific litigations, the discretionary amounts involved can be quite large. Yet, in fact, the determination of how to charge time is one of any law firm's most complex administrative problems. Few law firms have common policies; there are even differences between partners in the same firm. Despite what the phrase implies, time charging is very frequently *not* a simple mechanical matter of adding up the minutes and hours actually devoted to a client's exclusive business.

Negotiations in this area may be sensitive, but some aspects of it also should be undertaken during the retainer conference. At the least this will insure that thought is given to the matter and that uniform policies will be applied. It should also result in the equivalent of "most favored nation" treatment, the same as that accorded other key clients of the firm. It will always have the important effect of letting the firm know that the client is concerned that billings be what they should be.

The retainer discussion in this respect might begin with a request for the firm to outline its own policies. Thereafter, to the extent not covered, the following areas might be considered, together with any others suggested by the earlier statements:

1. *Minimum rates.* Frequently there is more than one time rate per attorney. Sometimes the lower rate will be for less-specialized work; sometimes for certain general retainer clients; sometimes for eleemosynary institutions. But sometimes there is no clear fixed policy, and the lower rate may be obtainable in large cases pretty much just by asking for it.

2. *Travel time.* How does the firm charge for travel? Is there a minimum for a day spent away from the office? What is it? What if work is done for another client en route, or time is devoted to matters (reading law journals) ordinarily charged to an office overhead account? What about weekends and holidays away from home, if no work is done? What about travel time spent for two or more clients, or to attend a bar association convention as well as to interview a witness for a client?

3. *Joint projects.* Where the same assignment is performed for two clients, how is the time divided? Is each charged in full? What if an earlier research project is simply updated?

4. *Rate revisions.* Will there be any changes in the rates during the period of the litigation? If so, on what basis are they usually revised? (*General* rate changes may be appropriate, reflecting inflation, normal anticipated salary increments, and the like. *Selective* rate changes, however, predicated on the importance of the attorney to the client, are questionable in the socioscientific litigation, where the client itself makes an enormous investment in educating attorneys in the policies and specialties involved. It is not at all uncommon for a law firm to agree in one of these larger cases that there will be no selective rate changes "for the duration," or for one, two, or three years.)

5. *Maximum hours.* Is there a maximum number of chargeable hours for any single day or other time period? If so, does it apply under all circumstances, or only some, such as while traveling or at trial? And does it apply to each client for which the attorney performs services during the period, or all combined? (Some firms or partners limit their hours to some maximum, such as ten hours per trial day, or ten hours per travel day except when the time actually worked is greater than ten hours apart from the time spent traveling.)

Just how many of the above questions one raises is obviously a matter requiring the exercise of considerable judgment and discretion. Good trial lawyers *are* hard to come by, and excesses may well create such reluctance as to persuade the firm to reject the proffered retainer. But corporate counsel is purchasing a very important and expensive service, and the amounts involved deserve attention. I once spent three months abroad working on a litigation for a client; it is not uncommon for a half dozen or more attorneys to be sent to remote parts of the world for similarly long periods on major matters. The out-of-town difference between a maximum ten-hour day, five-day week and a sixteen-hour day, five-day week, plus a standard ten-hour charge each for Saturday and Sunday, at the minimum $40 rate, is $2,000 per attorney per week!

Finally is the matter of disbursements, Item III on the litigation report. Ordinarily attorneys are quite specific and detailed in reporting disbursements—I have seen bills for a rounded $65,000 in professional services (always watch out for "rounded" figures) followed by $137.67 in disbursements, broken down even to specific telephone calls. This is also the smallest of the items involved, and by this time in the retainer discussions sensitivities may have been sufficiently aroused that one should rest on the statements in the form submitted and say nothing more.

For completeness in our discussion, it should be noted that the considerations involved in billing disbursements are not dissimilar to those in charging time: one trip can be taken for two clients; stenographic work done on overtime for a client might as easily have been accomplished during the daytime, and the daytime bar-association typing done at night. Who said that client A's work had to be done on a weekend, on overtime, and client B's on a weekday? Is first-class travel always authorized? Who pays for entertainment during a business trip? Are the expenses of spouses included on lengthy trips? Is there a charge for internal firm duplicating (sometimes a cost item amounting to thousands of dollars monthly), and what is it? How much general overhead is added? Is messenger or file or secretarial work handled as overhead or disbursement? Who pays for the trip taken jointly for client and professional (bar activity) purposes? The client may well be agreeable to all proposals, but if so it might just as well get credit for its beneficence. And once again, the fact that the client is concerned and aware and watching will inevitably have a favorable effect not only on the amounts charged, but in making it clear that the client remains very much in control.

In order to avoid any misunderstanding later on, the initial retainer discussion should also consider corporate counsel's other special rule-of-reason roles in aspects of the litigation. These are discussed elsewhere, and include particularly fact and company-witness preparation (Chapter 3), settlement (Chapter 5) and the staff attorney's participation in pretrial and at trial (Chapters 6 and 7). A trial attorney will ordinarily have no objection to corporate counsel's retainer indication of a desire to argue motions relating to certain issues, or to take certain depositions; but he or she may well view such a request made later as evidencing dissatisfaction or improper interference.

Exhibit 5 is a check list of matters that might be considered during the initial retainer discussion. It bears repetition that the

---

EXHIBIT 5

RETAINER DISCUSSION CHECK LIST

I. *Litigation Personnel*

   a. Identify, obtain specialty of, and if possible meet all attorneys to be assigned to case. Satisfied?

   b. All attorneys to understand rule-of-reason approach and know relevant basic client policies in major areas, such as with respect to civil rights, antitrust, and the environment.

   c. Single responsibility—attorney in charge of litigation should also be in charge of related internal firm administration and billing.

   d. Preference to be expressed for assignment of senior rather than junior attorneys, and for the same personnel to remain with litigation (and other client matters) throughout.

   e. No personnel changes without prior discussion.

II. *Litigation Strategy*

   a. Factual and legal research to be conducted at inception and philosophy of litigation determined so as to be consistent throughout.

   b. Memorandum to be prepared promptly following development of philosophy, setting forth anticipated trial tactics including timetable, specific discovery steps, motions, defenses, etc. To be revised *in writing* as appropriate so as always to be current. (See Exhibit 3.)

III. *Client Staff Participation*

    a. Client staff attorney to receive *advance* drafts of all significant documents (policy statements, pleadings, memoranda) in sufficient time to be able to participate fully in decisions.

    b. Client staff attorney routinely to receive copies of *all* other documents, including letters and internal legal memoranda.

    c. Client staff attorney to participate in all litigation planning and decisions, including even routine adjournments.

    d. Client staff attorney to participate in actual conduct of litigation to extent client wishes, including handling of depositions, arguing of motions, and even trying case or participating in the trial.

        1. *Ordinarily,* staff attorney will participate actively at least in the preparation of all client witnesses who testify.

        2. *Ordinarily,* client nonlegal personnel will handle all paraprofessional assignments (document searches, summaries, factual research, indexing, etc.).

IV. *Professional Charges*

    a. No contingency—fee to be based on time alone.

    b. Most-favored-nation treatment—lowest rate and time charges for each attorney.

    c. Policies as to time charges:

        1. How calculate travel and weekend time when away from home but no work, or work being done for other clients or matters?

        2. Any maximum per day?

        3. Any minimum per business day away from office? Per entry (1/10 hour, 1/4 hour, 1/2 hour)?

        4. Other? (E.g., reduction where attorney inefficient; increase where similar research just completed for another client; charging of training and education time, and of joint time spent traveling or conferring for other clients or purposes.)

    d. Regular (e.g., monthly or as predetermined amounts are reached) statements of time and charges to be furnished, broken down by attorney. (See Exhibit 4.)

    e. No changes in time rates during litigation (or perhaps other discrete period such as one year) without prior discussion.

    f. Policies as to disbursements:

      1. Internal duplication expense?

      2. Travel, meals, entertainment; first-class transportation; family transportation?

      3. Luncheon and dinner expense?

      4. Secretarial and other overtime?

      5. Expenses incurred for joint purposes on behalf of other clients or matters?

      6. Other? (e.g., publications, messenger, filing)?

    g. Disbursements to be charged only if required for client effort, *not* because of other firm or personal priorities (e.g., attorney or secretary working nights or weekends because of other client or bar activities during business day, not chargeable to client).

---

subjects may be sensitive ones, and that discretion must be exercised throughout in order to develop and maintain a fine professional relationship. Rarely would one discuss all these matters with any single firm or attorney at one time.

The Insured Litigation

Some comment is appropriate also regarding those cases in which the corporation's outside insurance carrier is involved and has insured the risk. This addition of another adversary element to the litigation can jeopardize the rule-of-reason approach. After all, the insurance company has only dollars at stake; it cannot be expected to have the same concern with general considerations of credibility as the corporation. Commonly it will have selected trial counsel from its own list of "acceptable" trial attorneys. Even though the client is the corporation, trial counsel knows that continuing business comes from the insurance company. Perceptions become even more attuned to "winning" the case at hand (or perhaps even a "package" of insurance cases being handled as a unit, apart from the specific merits of each), rather than the long-range benefit of the ultimate corporate client.

The corporation faced with the likelihood of ongoing socio-scientific litigations should be a self-insurer to a reasonable maximum. It should insure only the "catastrophic" loss that would otherwise mean disaster. These cases are already a regular part of the corporation's anticipated business, and it should prepare for them as it does any other routine matter. One should only insure against the unusual and the unanticipated.

Of course it is impossible to change overnight, and the reality of handling the defense of insured litigations will be with us for some time to come. It just makes the problems more difficult to solve, not impossible. If the matter is adequately presented, a carrier handling substantial and ongoing insurance claims will understand the desire of corporate counsel to participate in the selection of trial counsel in an important case and to be informed. It will at least try to work out ways in which the long-range interests of the company can be made to accord with the short-range objective of success in the particular case. If I am right that the rule-of-reason approach is in fact the lowest-risk approach to any major case, the carrier ultimately will welcome it. However, it is important that corporate counsel be ever alert to the inherent differences in perception.

It bears repetition with regard to all the matters considered in this chapter that every effort must be made throughout to preserve the vital professional relationship between trial and corporate counsel. Forms and procedures can be changed to meet the needs of any particular law firm or any special case; ordinarily direct and to-the-point approaches can be modified to adjust to anticipated sensitivity and recalcitrance. It would be most unfortunate if action taken to maximize results for the mutual corporate client were to interfere with the trial lawyer's necessary exercise of expertise—or result in no trial lawyer at all.

Settlement | Chapter 5

The conclusion of a dispute by voluntary measures—settlement—is another major area in which corporate counsel's litigation responsibility is primary to that of trial counsel. This is true even when the trial attorney has long been retained and the suit itself is well under way.

From the outset of the relationship with trial counsel, corporate counsel should make clear an intention to retain strict control of all aspects of settlement. It is the essence of corporate counsel's assignment to know the client's overall business as well as its strictly litigation concerns. No outside specialist can possibly be expected to understand the personalities and considerations as intimately, or to so sensitively and acutely make the requisite fine balancing of judgments, often with little time to act and less than complete knowledge.

The very different perceptions of trial and corporate counsel, referred to earlier, also are worth considering in this connection. Litigation is trial counsel's sole and exclusive business, day-in and day-out. This means that the existence of litigation is itself necessarily perceived differently by trial counsel. It does not deter the litigator from the main goal—it *is* the litigator's main goal. The precise opposite is true of corporate counsel, almost by definition. Litigation is a deterrent to his or her objectives. He or she may be unable to avoid it as a routine part of the company's business, but it most certainly is *not* the main business, and shouldn't be. Litigation is a necessary but undesired employment of corporate resources that could better be devoted to producing the goods or services which are the corporation's raison d'être. These conflicting realities greatly influence how each of the two counsel comes to judgments.

The trial lawyer, trained as an advocate and adversary, is constantly engaged in a struggle with the opposing party's attorney. Frequently this results in such strains of relationship or posturing that the flexibility and changes of pace needed to modify positions and develop new and different approaches to settlement are missing. Corporate counsel may be able to fill this breach.

Finally, ethical concerns preclude trial counsel from communicating directly with the opposing party, even when the adversary attorney seems deliberately to be placing improper obstacles in the path of settlement, or is so coloring reports of the discussions that negotiations are being frustrated. Even a written offer and statement of position may not get through unimpaired. Where corporate counsel and the client are fully informed, however, the client itself may conclude that direct discussions between the parties, without trial counsel being present, are in order. A meeting between corporate counsel or the chief executives themselves can be most productive, especially when both have been made to appreciate the waste of corporate resources that litigation entails. There is nothing improper in such direct client negotiations, at least if not procured by trial counsel for the purpose of outmaneuvering the adversary attorney.

To recommend that corporate counsel maintain primary responsibility for settlement and even conduct negotiations personally, however, is not to suggest that trial counsel be excluded in any respect. To the contrary, the trial attorney should continue fully informed here as in all other regards, and should ordinarily participate in the deliberations and even conduct the negotiations. His or her perceptions of the strengths and weaknesses of the client's case and the adversary position are essential to a realistic evaluation of any settlement proposals.

Most claims do not mature to litigations, of course, and usually settlement will have taken place before any trial lawyer is retained. The advantages of such early disposition have already been referred to; some insurance companies cite an aphorism that paying an automobile accident victim twice what is requested before an attorney is retained (which is twice what the victim thinks the case is worth!) will result in a settlement at an amount one-half that of any later figure—without considering the costs of litigation at all. There is much merit to this, and the earliest reasonable settlement should always be an objective.

It should perhaps be added by way of caution that even a

formal release can be set aside in many jurisdictions if there has been any overreaching or other improper advantage taken of a victim—particularly when a substantial corporation has been dealing with an uninformed individual. This is the so-called "little old lady" settlement, but is rarely a problem in the major socioscientific cases. In any event, pressing too hard for an advantageous settlement—or any benefit—can be a serious tactical mistake. Twisting the knife too hard after it has struck home may make it come out.

Tactics

Settlement negotiation of the rule-of-reason litigation is simply another aspect of settlement and corporate negotiation generally, albeit made somewhat more difficult by the antagonism so commonly incident to litigations. There is no common pattern to success, but a great number of different (and varying) considerations to keep in mind. Central to proper handling, as elsewhere, is an understanding of the dispute from the viewpoint of the adversary. (Another aphorism holds that neither side is happy with a good settlement.) Certain special considerations apply to rule-of-reason settlement tactics, however, which call for separate discussion.

Litigation Costs

Should anticipated litigation costs be added to or subtracted from the estimated outcome on the merits in computing an offer of settlement? Clearly such costs are a relevant factor. In the major socioscientific case, they can be much higher than the dollar amounts involved in the dispute directly in issue (although of course they should never be more than involved in its long-range consequences.) Yet adversary costs are likely to be very much the same. And if costs are blindly included in settlement proposals, the result will be to pay all but the most flagrant and outlandish claims (which presumptively can be gotten rid of by quick court application at low expense.) This in turn might encourage the bringing of unjustified cases.

The most that can be said, therefore, is that trial counsel's probably different perception of litigation expense should be understood; all the litigation costs (of both sides) should be estimated as precisely as possible in connection with any settlement negotiations; and these amounts should be given prominent consideration in evaluating any proposals.

Other Litigant Relations

It is quite common for there to be customer, supplier, or other ongoing relationships between the litigating parties to the socioscientific case. The adversary litigant, for example, may be an important supplier or a large customer. Should the risk of prejudicing such a desirable relationship be considered in settlement? Or, if the adversary is dependent on the client's business, should continuation of that business be held out as an inducement or its cut-off as a threat?

Here the answer is clearer. The business personnel involved in the commercial aspects of the problem have permitted it to deteriorate to the point of legal dispute, and the attorneys involved should do their best to exclude commercial concerns of this kind from their thinking. Corporate counsel should make clear to the business personnel at the outset that the litigation will be conducted pretty much independently of these relationships, letting the "chips fall where they may." And that's the way it should be handled from then on. A party cannot conduct an effective litigation if continually worrying about whether the adversary will resort to some outside, nonlitigation power, or anticipating the use of such a power if things don't go well.

In larger companies with dominant market positions, antitrust concerns are necessarily involved in the use of market power in one respect to influence commercial conduct in another. Moreover, such use of totally unrelated power as a weapon or threat is suggestive of a lack of confidence in the merits of one's case and might later be used as damaging evidence.

Finally, these *a priori* commercial judgments by attorneys can be quite wrong. I have seen a tight-supply picture relaxed considerably following suit by a customer, for example, because of the supplier's concern that any rationing or restriction might backfire on the case itself, unless clearly and obviously justified by non-litigating considerations.

The foregoing discussion assumes that the business personnel have done their best to resolve the matter commercially before letting it deteriorate to litigation. This assumption is not always justified, of course. If corporate counsel considers that the nonlegal employees have not done their job properly, the remedy should *not* be to assume nonlegal functions, but to see that appropriate internal corporate corrective action is taken.

This approach of concentrating on the litigation considerations and "letting the chips fall where they may" applies even when the adversary litigant is a government agency that has vital and continuing power over the client's business. The rule-of-reason settlement approach discussed at the end of this chapter may help a business to avoid some of these litigations and minimize adversary antagonism, but otherwise there is no way of effectively asserting an adversary litigation position if constrained by fear of some nonlitigation retaliation. Should the adversary do something improper, it may be subject to attack in the same fashion as the corporation for such tactics.

Confidences

It is rather common in settlement discussions for business and legal personnel to try to deal with adversaries "off-the-record" or "without prejudice," and otherwise accept promises from each other that if the negotiations fail, neither side will make reference to what has been said and done in any subsequent dealings. Both sides may honestly intend to do this, but it simply cannot be. As with all other elements in rule-of-reason litigations, what one says and does even in the most private and confidential of settlement negotiations must be with the knowledge that it may later be disclosed. As the hostile witness referred to earlier, for example, an adversary may perceive settlement statements as efforts at blackmail or otherwise improper and may seek remedial action. Quite commonly a judge or other trier of fact at some later point in the litigation will inquire regarding what settlement discussions have taken place, and an answer must be given. If one exhibits a confidential or privileged document to an adversary during a settlement disclosure, the adversary cannot be expected to disregard it if a witness later contradicts its contents. The courts even permit a criminal prosecutor to use unlawfully obtained evidence in certain kinds of cross-examination of the criminal defendant.

"Playing it too close to the vest," however, can severely inhibit settlement. If the atmosphere is conducive to negotiations and corporate counsel appreciates the risks of future use of disclosure against the corporation, a direct, frank, open, rule-of-reason approach is the one most likely to succeed. The old saws precluding disclosures of anything but trivia, demanding that settlement be postponed until one is at one's strongest, prohibiting the making of a first offer as a "sign of weakness," and warning not to "bid against yourself," all have elements of truth to them, of course. But often, making the initial offer in fact evidences strength and conviction, and reducing one's own earlier offer evidences an honest willingness to weigh adversary disclosures, which can be quite disarming. Both sides cannot be at their strongest points at the same time; someone *has* to make the first offer and someone *has* to give if there is to be a rapprochement.

Ongoing Preparation

All too frequently attorneys look at settlement negotiations as a means of avoiding work. They even come to the settlement discussions inadequately prepared on the facts and law, and stop all other litigation preparation as soon as negotiations have begun in earnest. This is poor tactics.

Although on occasion some of the more antagonistic or expensive aspects of pretrial might be postponed briefly during the height of settlement discussions, generally the litigation should proceed on schedule. Remember that the business interests are presumed to have exhausted their efforts at amicable resolution before the matter reached the litigation stage, and it is therefore the existence of the litigation which has generated the more receptive atmosphere.

It also requires a high degree of conceit to believe that one can dispose of a difficult matter where others have tried so hard by bluffing or "playing by ear." Never bluff; always be ready to proceed if one's hand is called. Settlement discussions furnish an important opportunity; unsuccessful negotiations, however, waste much time, effort, and money. One should come to the meetings fully prepared, knowing one's strengths and weaknesses and alternatives, and as much of the adversary case as possible. If the court litigation has not yet begun, for example, the complaint should at least have been drafted and might have even been printed. The small cost is trivial in comparison to the knowledge obtained— and the inevitable impact on the adversary distinguishing reality from bluff. If the litigation is under way, there is ordinarily no reason to stop internal preparation, which will enhance the litigation position if the settlement discussions fail, as they most frequently do. Even the adversary aspects might continue, for there is much waste to stopping and starting. I have seen litigations proceed for years, at huge expense, with little progress towards trial because so much time was devoted to settlement.

Continued progress toward trial is also an important inducemant to settlement. Most cases are in fact settled "on the courthouse steps," partly reflecting the fact that the parties are so often unwilling to make decisions until the realities of trial and final judgment are obvious and unavoidable (plus the unjustified fear of trial, to be discussed later in Chapter 7).

Outside Assistance

Where trial counsel cannot effect a settlement, corporate counsel sometimes can; where corporate counsel cannot, executive personnel sometimes can. Sometimes, however, individuals even more remote to the litigation are needed, who can approach the issues with fresh minds and fewer preconceptions. The use of formal mediation and conciliation services, where available, can be helpful. (These are quite commonly employed in labor and marital disputes, for example.) Such intervention need not be formal, however. Not infrequently both parties will accept a respected public or private figure as an intermediary or go-between. He or she will have no authority other than persuasion, but may be able to exert a powerful influence and can furnish the parties some protection against any subsequent misuse of settlement disclosures by withholding details and revealing only conclusions. His or her role can differ substantially from that of the trial judge in the litigation itself (who today also more and more commonly seeks to encourage settlement), because the parties see the judge as the final arbiter of the litigation and accordingly maintain their litigation postures before him.

Arbitration

Arbitration as a form of third-party participation deserves special treatment, because the arbitrator has the authority to enter a binding judgment which the courts will enforce and from which only the most limited kinds of appeal will be successful. It is thus a kind of quasi-judicial proceeding.

Arbitration requires a voluntary submission of the dispute by agreement of the parties in advance of the controversy or thereafter. Once the agreement is made, however, either party can enforce it. Although the agreement need not be in any special form, it is quite common today for the parties to use the forms, rule, and procedures of the American Arbitration Association (AAA), operating nationwide with headquarters in New York City. The AAA maintains a panel of qualified people willing to serve as arbitrators.

Arbitration has become quite common in certain types of corporate transactions, such as brokerage and labor disputes, and may provide partial answers to the burgeoning medical malpractice problem. Most corporations, however, do not consider arbitration a suitable method for the disposition of other kinds of claims. This is a mistake.

Arbitration has its limitations for the corporate party. Arbitrators frequently have a tendency to compromise and balance equities. Judges and jurors also compromise, of course, but where there are strong legal or factual points, special rulings and specific findings of fact and conclusions of law can be sought from a judge, and special verdicts from a jury, which limit the effects of compromise. This is not usually possible with an arbitrator who knows his business. Accordingly the company with a strong legal case (such as a good statute-of-limitations or statute-of-frauds defense) may well do better in a judicial court, where one or two reviews of an erroneous legal decision are possible. In addition, the cost of litigation (usually but not always lower in arbitration) is not ordinarily as significant to the corporate as to the individual litigant.

But arbitration *can* be a most useful tool for settlement of some kinds of corporate litigations. Punitive damages are sometimes the corporate party's most serious concern. I have never seen an arbitration award of punitive or exemplary damages, and doubt its validity in most jurisdictions (at least if the award identifies this as one of its components). Arbitrators honored by selection on an AAA panel tend to be members of the "Establishment" and more sympathetic to vested property rights and interests than most juries and many politically selected judges. They rarely award the huge amounts returned by lay juries or judges accustomed to large verdicts. It may be possible by arbitration to avoid the dangerous jurisdiction of a foreign court. If time is important, one can usually complete an arbitration proceeding more quickly than a judicial one.

Many adversaries know all this, of course. But they still sometimes can be persuaded to accept the jurisdiction of an arbitration tribunal in order to avoid the need to retain (and share fees) with outside trial counsel, or to get a quick and inexpensive decision, or for some other special reason.

If and when arbitration has been agreed upon by formal contract, the litigation proceeds much as any other, subject of course to the applicable special rules. Arbitration is no more the universal litigation panacea than anything else, but should always be considered when exploring the range of alternatives for resolving a dispute.

Finality of Settlement

One of the most difficult tasks in settling the major socioscientific litigation is to develop a mechanism to assure (as much as possible) that the same case will not crop up again the next day, someplace else, brought by a different party. The dangers of destroying evidence or of access to evidence have already been discussed; limiting third-party access to the materials without actual destruction can sometimes be achieved by transferring them to the control of the concerned litigant, but here the materials still continue subject to reach in future discovery proceedings. Contractual restraints limiting the right of a settling party or its counsel to help others in future cases tend to be regarded as against public policy, and are often unenforceable legally as well as practically.

This is a tough problem and sometimes will prove insoluble— the matter will just have to proceed on to trial and final judgment, and even then there will be no certainty. But sometimes the assistance of the trial judge or administrative tribunal can be helpful in fashioning remedies that will have at least some general application to third parties. Formally entered determinations, including findings of fact, may place serious obstacles in the paths of new and separate claims of the same kind. For this reason, and because the judicial or administrative arbiter frequently considers himself or herself as much concerned as the parties with disposition short of trial, it is usually good practice to involve the arbiter in the settlement negotiations at as early a point as is consistent with the success of the negotiations, and before the terms and conditions have become *faits accomplis*.

Adversary Relations

Sometimes during settlement negotiations in rule-of-reason cases (or in other parts of the litigation process) it will become apparent that an adversary or his or her attorney is acting in an improper way. The conduct is not explainable as the result of different perceptions of the same facts, but is caused by improper motivation or ethical impropriety which makes it clear that further efforts at good-faith dealings are unjustified and unwise. Fortunately this kind of conduct is rare, but it may become more common in early rule-of-reason cases in which some "sporting" trial attorneys will regard the rule-of-reason approach as naive tactics to be taken advantage of. When it does occur, the response must be quick and positive. All further informal dealings should be terminated and communication with the party and counsel made only in writing or on the record. If telephone calls cannot be refused, they should be followed up by "confirming" letters setting forth precisely what happened and requesting response if exception is to be taken. Stipulations should not only set forth the precise action agreed upon but also recite the request which gave rise to the agreement and any other information which may later be controverted. The practice of writing contemporaneous memoranda to the client to make clear that the client is proceeding on counsel's advice and therefore not acting out of improper personal motivation should be encouraged in an effort to avoid unfounded charges based upon allegedly informal settlement disclosures or otherwise. The arbiter once again should be involved as much in the proceedings as possible, so that he or she will understand also why it is necessary to act in this fashion and may ultimately initiate corrective action. On occasion, resort to a judicial or bar association grievance procedure may be appropriate, although this is itself so commonly a "sporting" litigation tactic that it should be employed only in the extreme case where misconduct cannot seriously be controverted.

The Rule-of-Reason Settlement

One new and quite different approach to settlement should be considered in appropriate major socioscientific litigations in which the rule of reason is to be applied. This is to disclose the full case to the adversary at the inception, "no holds barred," preferably in a formal way, with witnesses, fact and law memoranda, and even voluntary submission to cross-examination.

Consider the plight of the government agency honestly seeking to apply a new and untested statute. It is subject to pressures and inputs from a great variety of sources, legislative, consumer and public, as well as industry. Its working personnel, by and large, are few and spread thin; many are quite uneducated in the complex facts and sciences involved. They have learned to mistrust their outside sources because the perceptions presented are so distorted and the positions taken so extreme. They have heard environmentalists claim that a given course of action will destroy a natural resource, or kill wildlife or humans; but they have also listened to industry claim that the alternative will compel withdrawal of a product from the market, or throw large numbers of people out of work, or seriously reduce the national product. These dire warnings of disaster have not materialized in the past and the employees working on the matter cannot assume they will occur now just because the assertion is made, nor know whose prediction to choose.

Wouldn't it be impressive if such government personnel were given something they *could* trust? If one really believes, why not present one's views to them in full, in a form the credibility of which cannot be controverted, which invites question in uncertain areas, and which promises considered response where an answer is not known? If the course of action proposed is as unwise as the company believes, it ought to be able to convince reasonable people of that fact—if it does so before positions have become frozen and change thereby made difficult and perhaps impossible. The only loss is the tactical disadvantage of early disclosure of material which must later be furnished anyway. This is a small price to pay for the many possible advantages.

As applied to settlement, the rule-of-reason approach in these circumstances would call for the corporation to furnish a formal submission to the agency concerned, setting forth its contentions and supporting evidence in a comprehensive and substantial fashion. The submission would contain a request for an informal hearing, at which counsel for the company would present arguments orally and respond to any questions which might be asked, either immediately or after subsequent research or analysis. It would also propose to have the testimony of witnesses furnished in advance, in writing, with the witnesses available at the hearing to answer any questions that might be posed or consider conducting any further investigations which might be indicated. It would recite that the agency is not asked to make any arguments or submit anything in response, or do anything except have the appropriate decision makers listen, although the corporation would welcome any materials which might be submitted at any time in an effort to identify areas of concern or difference. Assuming the offer is accepted, at the appointed day the company's attorneys and its witnesses would appear and present their information fully and openly.

Needless to say, the proposal for a rule-of-reason settlement must be cast in sufficiently persuasive form so as to make it very clear that the corporation means business and is not coming hat in hand, begging for charity. It might well be printed and bound, and in any event should contain all the legal analyses and factual presentations incident to a strong legal claim.

Sometimes the number of parties will be so many and the interests and objectives so diffuse that the creation of a vehicle for negotiation will be an essential preliminary to any settlement approach. Just how this can be accomplished must depend on the particular facts and circumstances of each case, but always it will require that the initiating party begin by encouraging the development of a limited number of groups of parties aligned with each other generally in interest, and then obtaining the needed authority to negotiate, using the techniques discussed in the section on joint preparation in Chapter 6.

The benefits of the rule-of-reason settlement approach are several. It makes it possible to work out a settlement at the earliest possible time, before official decisions have been made and actions taken from which retreat may be construed as defeat. The more one can persuade afresh rather than compel another to change, the more likely an effective compromise. It is no more wise to make an adversary admit error than to corner a ferocious tiger—he may be forced to fight, perhaps to his death, but also to the serious injury of his attacker. This mandate, along with those requiring that an opponent be furnished an "exit with honor" and permitted to save face whenever possible, is litigation dogma.

The rule-of-reason approach encourages and maximizes the possibility of early settlement. Even if total agreement is not reached, at least some issues probably will have been resolved and other problems clarified and pinpointed. Perhaps equally important, it also makes it possible to discover any defects in one's own analysis before the course of the litigation has become charted. Socioscientific cases are extremely difficult and present great risk to the corporate party; even the best preparation may have overlooked some consideration beyond one's own perception. By discovering any adverse reaction or response in this early session, the company can fashion its best presentation for the later public dispute, should settlement prove impossible.

A rule-of-reason settlement approach also minimizes the adversary antagonism inherent in the dispute. As stated earlier in this chapter, government agencies can have enormous power over the modern corporation, and other relationships must continue even while the most intensive litigations are pending. Understanding associations should be encouraged to the maximum extent possible.

Finally, a rule-of-reason approach begins the record of the dispute in the manner most conducive to credibility and successful final outcome. Assuming the dispute is not resolved at this point, evidence of the presentation will be helpful in convincing the ultimate arbiter of the corporation's conviction in its presentation and of its integrity of purpose—consistency in approach will enhance credibility. If the opposition later produces a response not disclosed at the initial meetings, its value will be impaired as having been developed *post litem motam,* or its credibility and motivation will come into question for "sandbagging." For all these reasons the effort is almost a "no lose" affair, as calculated to meet the challenge of socioscientific litigation from the corporate litigant's perspective as the environmentalist's "no-win" approach (discussed in Chapter 1) is designed to fit that perspective. In one case, for example, the approach resulted in a compromise that was completely satisfactory to the litigant, at minimum expense. At the same time, another litigant following the traditional approach was able to obtain partially similar relief only after lengthy litigation, including appeal, at enormous expense, loss of discretionary government benefits, and unnecessarily impaired relationships with regulatory authorities.

The rule-of-reason settlement approach is not appropriate to every socioscientific litigation. Unfortunately, for some time to come many adversaries will be far too antagonistic to be persuaded, and too transitory or otherwise beyond reach to be compelled to reveal even the "time of day" in response. All they can be expected to do is to reshape their contentions in the most adversary fashion possible to meet the rule-of-reason presentation. The approach's greatest utility will surely be with the major government agencies, and this should be where it begins. But here and there an effort might also be commenced with a more responsible civil rights or environmental organization. Perhaps, sooner or later, a two-way channel can be opened which will lead to sound, negotiated, voluntary resolutions of these disputed matters, in the public interest and without the necessity for resorting to a litigation process unsuited to these kinds of issues.

Pretrial Preparation

Chapter **6**

This chapter and the next deal with those aspects of the litigation process in which trial counsel's role is primary: the balance of pretrial preparation, trial, and appeal. Even in these areas, however, corporate counsel seeking to apply the rule-of-reason approach has most important parallel responsibilities: He or she must see to it that the corporation's long-range program is properly considered in all decisions, and must be able to decide matters on which there is a legitimate difference of opinion or approach. Quick, decisive action on those issues where corporate counsel's role continues to be primary, such as with respect to settlement or parts of fact preparation, is essential. Continuing surveillance of the work of trial counsel to see that it remains of top quality and is handled as economically and efficiently as possible must be maintained. Although corporate counsel's knowledge and expertise in many of these areas need not be as extensive as in the litigation respects considered in earlier chapters, he or she must still know what to expect and how to distinguish the bad from the good.

These next two chapters will try to point out where the rule-of-reason approach calls for a modification of normal trial strategy, or where there are different schools of thought among trial lawyers. An effort will also be made to identify the important pretrial, trial, and appellate considerations, so that corporate counsel will have an idea of what to expect and what questions to ask. The chapters are not intended to serve as a primer on tactics and strategy, however. Corporate counsel has a critical management role in the functions discussed, but he or she must leave the details to the trial expert. The trial attorney is a specialist and should not be required to explain every move in depth or be so closely controlled and supervised that the occasional but still vital opportunities for display of genius are lost.

There are probably as many different ways of trying a case as there are trial lawyers. It is important that corporate counsel employing the rule-of-reason approach at an early point discuss with trial counsel the need to adhere to the three fundamental rules of litigation strategy considered briefly in connection with corporate counsel's primary preparation responsibilities: the affirmative approach, maintaining litigation control, and the avoidance of unnecessary delay. Some further discussion of these strategies is necessary before turning to the specific pretrial issues.

The Affirmative Approach

If corporate counsel has properly instructed witnesses and carried on the requisite investigation, the corporation's affirmative explanation of its conduct will have at least been outlined by the time trial counsel enters the picture. The permutations and combinations of the facts are infinite, but at the heart will be a simply stated exposition of why the corporation's actions and position are in the public interest—why "we" are the "good guys." In the typical risk-benefit environmental contest, for example, it will be to emphasize the public benefits of the company's product or service, even if the only charges relate to anticipated risks and harm.

Trial counsel should be asked to emphasize this affirmative story in every action taken, from the first pleading and appearance before the arbiter on. He or she should be requested to design the structure of the litigation so that this aspect must be focused on by others as well. This may call for the filing of a counterclaim, the making of a motion, or the taking of some other formal procedural step. The trial attorney should instruct his or her associates and colleagues to do the same, so that continued, consistent repetition from the beginning ultimately will define the validity of this issue as a key matter to be litigated at the hearing.

Some counsel may respond that there is no affirmative in the case presented, or that the posture of the litigation has previously been so defined by others, that the proposed affirmative cannot be made an issue. These are not valid responses.

There is *always* an affirmative, however hard it may be to dig out. With the exception of those very few individuals who should be institutionalized, everyone justifies his own conduct to himself. In over a quarter century of trial practice, including criminal defense and prosecution of even the most hardened criminals, I can honestly say: "I've never met a bad criminal," just as Father Flanagan of Boy's Town so often repeated: "I've never met a bad boy." The justification in the latter kinds of cases (societal mistreatment, poor parental training, hunger, and the like) frequently may not constitute a legal excuse or defense, but it evokes sympathy and always presents the facts in the best possible light for the proponent. Maximum favorable self-perception is as characteristic of the corporate party as of the individual.

Trial counsel see all kinds of cases over the years, and understandably may become somewhat cynical. In a sense, corporate counsel must sell the trial lawyer on the merits of the case, at least initially. The more trial counsel is convinced, the better will be his or her preparation and presentation. Emphasis of the affirmative is in some respects just another way of saying that the facts should be adduced in the manner most sympathetic to their proponent. Phrased thus, it must be obvious that there will inevitably be a most sympathetic (as well as a least sympathetic) case. To suggest that the litigation precludes this would be in effect to deny the litigant his constitutional day in court. The affirmative is really just his defense, expressed in the best possible manner.

In the typical corporate socioscientific case, in contrast to the individual criminal litigation, the societal rules are still being developed and presentation of the affirmative will ordinarily result in at least a partially favorable verdict. If such a presentation cannot be developed—if there is simply no possible version of the facts which will evoke public sympathy or appear in the public interest—then the rule of reason demands that the corporation withdraw from the fray. Only a miscarriage of justice could help, and that should never be the objective of any responsible system of dispute resolution.

Maintenance of Control

The second litigation strategy that corporate counsel should ask trial counsel to continue is maintenance of maximum possible control of the case. This means assuming the initiative whenever possible, anticipating what others will do and moving first, being always ready, asking for delay or postponement only when *in extremis,* and acting as an aggrieved plaintiff or proponent even though styled a defendant. In some cases, of course, this is easier said than done. The opposition will have initiated the claim and be moving aggressively forward on all fronts. But more often than not, a party that wants and is prepared to assume the burden and expense can take over. Litigation is costly and trial lawyers are a busy lot. If one moves forward as fast as possible, insisting that the substantial time periods between formal litigation steps be utilized fully, it is usually possible to far outdistance the opposition in preparation. If one's own visual aids are ready for the first motion, for example, rather than prepared only for trial purposes as is common, the court will use them for reference, perhaps from that point forward. If an accurate glossary is supplied with the initial law or fact memorandum, albeit phrased sympathetically to one's case, that may become the standard terminology of the litigation. Voluntarily undertaking and supplying the initial legal research establishes a framework into which others must fit, or show cause to change; furnishing document and fact controls and indices works in the same fashion. Undertaking the litigation-control burdens for the court or an adversary is as effective a tactic as preparing the first draft is for the corporate contract negotiator. The stage is set, and the burden is on the opponent to explain why modification is needed. The preparer knows what went into the design; others can only guess.

Requests for delay for personal reasons or to accommodate other commitments constitute "due bills" for future call. If one does not seek them unnecessarily and grants them where appropriate, within the limits discussed below, one gradually builds up a reservoir of "calls" which can be most useful in other connections at other times.

Litigation procedure has many variations and the purpose of maintaining control is to be able to shape that procedure in the fashion most sympathetic to one's affirmative case. This may result in being able to appear before a more understanding arbiter, or select a time for trial when the atmosphere is most acceptable, or formulate fact and law controls most likely to encourage the desired result. The details cannot be anticipated even in a specific case, but maintenance of control invariably maximizes the possibilities of success.

Avoiding Delay

The third litigation strategy to be communicated to trial counsel is to avoid unnecessary delay. The word "unnecessary" is to be emphasized, because delay is often required to achieve other overriding litigation strategies, such as the development of an affirmative presentation. But delay is to be requested or accepted only if positively justified by some other more important consideration. Trial counsel should not be permitted to engage in the commonplace and almost routine practice of exchanging professional "courtesies" to accommodate vacation and personal schedules and other conveniences. He or she may grant these extensions when they serve a purpose, including even professional courtesy, within limits, but should staff up so that his or her own needs for them are kept to the absolute minimum.

Avoiding delay is of course one way of maintaining control of the litigation. Its importance in that respect has already been indicated. In addition, aggressive progress towards ultimate conclusion is a sign of confidence in the merits of one's own contentions, and is therefore very much a part of the rule-of-reason approach to corporate credibility. Finally, it minimizes litigation expense. There is some unavoidable minimum of legal preparation required in any case, but almost no maximum in the major socioscientific litigation. One can go on and on exploring the details of the benefits and the risks and the alternatives, and *their* alternatives, substantially ad infinitum. A measure of what one must do, of course, is what the other side has done. If there is time and the other side conducts research for another rodent generation or two, or for several more months, one must do the same, no matter that the materiality of the work is suspect. The trial-law principle that time gets filled up with work is worth repeating; in the socioscientific litigation, this work can become so expensive that limiting the time becomes a goal in itself.

Most trial attorneys will not be accustomed to corporate counsel requesting the right to participate even in the granting of the customary professional courtesies; some may resent it. But if the substantial objectives sought are explained and discussed, as they must be, usually there should be no problem reaching understanding even in this area.

We turn now to a consideration of a number of other specific pretrial areas with which corporate counsel should be concerned. No common substantive theme or pattern joins these together, and they will be discussed in the rough chronological order in which they usually take place.

Publicity

The public ultimately decides the major socioscientific issues, and publicity regarding the litigation is therefore of great importance. The desirability of having a person skilled in public information on the litigation team has already been outlined, and that person's participation with trial counsel is of continuing significance.

Publicity regarding pending cases has become a very sensitive subject in recent years. Although cases now have begun to spell out the guidelines, great care must be taken to avoid violating as yet still undefined and uncertain rules, applied differently by different arbiters in different courts. At one time, the only serious publicity problem related to the jury case, where jury access to evidence not presented through the judicial process might violate the rights of the parties. Judges were considered quite capable of excluding such matters from their considerations, and even today will write opinions stating that inadmissible evidence has not influenced their decision.

Despite First Amendment concerns, there is a more modern tendency to consider that publicity seeking to encourage public support for a given course of action is improper if participated in by a party to a pending litigation, even if the case is a nonjury one or pending on appeal before only judges. In one important socioscientific litigation pending before a single judge, for example, a specific order to this effect was entered. It reads in pertinent part as follows:

> The parties having been heard and the Court being duly advised, in the interest of justice and accurate, objective, dispassionate and fair comment and news reporting of the proceedings in this action, it is hereby
>
> ORDERED that plaintiff and defendant are restricted from disseminating news of any proceeding before this Court or of any matters relating to this action by press release, press conference or interview with the press, without the consent of the Court.
>
> All of the proceedings before this Court in this action, unless otherwise ordered upon written motion for good cause shown, shall be open to any member of the news media and any member of the public. All information concerning such proceedings shall be obtained by representatives of the press or by the public by attendance at such proceedings, or from the documents and transcripts of the proceedings on file in the office of the Clerk of this Court.
>
> Plaintiff and defendant may make available to the press or to the public a copy of any document, or permit the inspection of any transcript, which is on file with this Court, and may advise the press or public of the existence of such materials, but are prohibited from commenting on or characterizing such documents or transcripts, or the information contained therein, without the permission of the Court. It is the intent of this provision that the documents and transcripts on file in the office of the Clerk of this Court shall speak for themselves

with respect to all proceedings in this action, and it is also the intent of this provision that neither party shall initiate contacts with the press or volunteer information with respect to this action.

The provisions of this Order shall apply to all persons who have any responsibility for, or who are in any way involved in, the handling of this action, including all potential witnesses or consultants employed by either party."*

The order was sustained on attack by third parties, ruled to be without standing to complain. Although thereafter modified in various respects and finally withdrawn, it reflects a judicial concern with publicity which must be considered even in the nonjury case.

The preparation and dissemination of litigation publicity is a function of the corporation's public-information personnel, not its inside or outside lawyers. Public information (not public "relations," a phrase coming into disrepute because of its implications of information "management" and contrivance) is a specialty calling for training and experience as much as any other. Moreover, as a general rule the last thing clients want is publicity—for their attorneys, that is. People want to see their own names in the press, not their representatives or agents, at least if the information is favorable. An attorney who personally participates in public comment, therefore, is not only running the risk of infringing ethical standards, but of displeasing his or her client as well.

Trial counsel should always be consulted before any publicity is released. He or she is the expert on the anticipated reaction of the arbiter and the local community and will have to answer for any misconduct that might be suggested. Trial counsel should be able to assist in the preparation of comments most suited to serving the many litigation objectives involved.

The trial lawyer who is experienced in socioscientific cases

---

* Pretrial Order No. 4, United States v. IBM, Civ. 69–200 (S.D.N.Y. May 12, 1972).

should understand the new judicial concern with publicity designed to stimulate public support. If not, corporate counsel must explain the problem and all its implications. Some trial counsel, perhaps once burned, will caution against *any* public comment. Here it will be the responsibility of corporate counsel to explain the broad sweep of the socioscientific issues involved, the fact that the immediate litigation is only one battle along the way (and often a relatively minor one at that), and that the ultimate answers will come only from proper public understanding and response. If trial counsel continues recalcitrant, the possibility of obtaining advice from the court or local bar association should be considered. Only in the most unusual situation should corporate counsel permit publicity to proceed without the invaluable guidance and assistance of trial counsel.

Choice of Forum

Quite often there will be a wide choice of places in which the socioscientific dispute can be litigated. The parties involved are likely to be multinational and the issues nationwide or even worldwide; many local and federal courts will have jurisdiction, as well as different regional offices of different administrative agencies. Selection of the forum in which the chances for success are greatest, assuming the die has not already been cast by the opposition and cannot be changed, may be a quite challenging task, requiring the balancing of a great variety of considerations.

Patent lawyers know how much the federal circuits differ in their attitudes towards patents and commonly rush to the most favorable. There are equally favorable and unfavorable environmental, antitrust, and civil-rights courts. Sometimes the race to select is almost embarrassing. Counsel will watch the lower tribunal clerk's office, waiting for the decision to be filed, with an open telephone line to a colleague at a distant appellate court so as to be able to file the first appeal. The fight in the higher courts may turn on who's clock was right and who filed a few seconds or minutes ahead of the other, which in turn determines which appellate court decides the case.

It may be a sad commentary on our judicial system that decisions turn so much on the attitudes of human judges and administrators, but that is the way it is and the differences must be reckoned with. Choice of forum therefore requires that the substantive and procedural law of each applicable jurisdiction be analyzed, calendar delay examined, local attitudes considered, arbiters evaluated, and the myriad other relevant issues treated. Trial counsel's judgments may be crucial, yet often of course the selection of trial counsel will itself depend on the forum chosen. In such cases, a number of potential trial counsel must be consulted, with corporate counsel given the added task of evaluating the extent to which any judgments might have been influenced by a subconscious wish to be, or not to be, retained for the litigation itself.

One aspect of forum choice deserves elucidation—the adverse judicial reaction to what is often called "forum shopping." Although judges and administrative arbiters know the practice exists, and even appreciate and acknowledge its applicability to others, most resent the suggestion that they might have been selected on this ground. Each perceives himself or herself as impartial and unprejudiced and quite able to render a decision without fear or favor. In addition, as part of the justice dispensing system, they understandably react adversely to this reflection of its inequities and dependence upon human failings. I have seen, for example, a judge uniformly considered "easy" in sentencing criminals in white-collar crime cases respond with a substantial prison term when defense counsel had too obviously maneuvered to get the case before him. Although the judge was clearly not conscious of his motivation, everyone else in the courtroom was.

Excessive "forum shopping" should be avoided for another reason as well. The opposition must be anticipated to have the same ability to judge good and bad jurisdictions, and therefore to make a later motion to dismiss based on *forum non conveniens,* or a motion to change venue or to transfer. A demonstration of obvious "shopping" will help win such an application for the opponent, with the desired forum lost and the new forum prejudiced even further by the evidence of "shopping." Accordingly, there should be some legitimate and reasonable explanation for the choice of any forum wholly apart from the proclivities of the legal arbiter and tribunal. This explanation should be well documented in advance of the attack, so as to be able to establish that it was not just dreamed up in answer to a charge.

In the major socioscientific disputes, there will almost always be a number of different jurisdictions having the requisite significant points of contact: corporate headquarters or headquarters of the opposition, manufacturing locations, major sales and use areas, concentrations of research or witnesses, and localities of great public interest or concern. Sometimes the very lack of public clamor can be referred to as a proper reason for choosing a forum, in that only there can one expect a fair and impartial public hearing. Much can be done to help establish the needed contacts, such as by carefully selecting the places in which expert witnesses and investigators are retained and in which research and other investigations are conducted. Selection of a frequently retained trial counsel on whom one has relied in the past and who is located in the forum of choice is quite useful. Judges dislike interference with a client's choice of attorney, and often are reluctant to take action which interferes with the local law practice. There is nothing improper with any of this, provided there are legitimate reasons for the action and they are not contrived or distorted so as to create an invalid presentation.

Procedure

Every tribunal has a set of procedural rules to govern its actions, and most are written and relatively simple and short. These rules are of enormous importance to the conduct of the proceeding and sometimes can be determinative. The stories of senators and representatives who achieve important objectives by procedural strategy are legion, and yet only suggestive of what can be done when the rules are adequately digested in the far more complex litigation.

Eminent trial counsel who move from tribunal to tribunal are able to pick up and apply the different sets of rules without much trouble, and corporate counsel should do the same. Such rules map the future course of a case and suggest the inquiries to make and the things to watch for. Surprisingly, many attorneys, including counsel to the administrative agencies in which the very matters at issue may be pending, do not bother to examine them in any depth, so that such knowledge can constitute a significant tactical advantage. Even more often, experienced attorneys and arbiters will continue to apply the stricter procedural rules of yesteryear, so that use of the more liberal modern revisions will permit one to take advantage of the changes without suffering the disbenefits. Failure to study the local procedural rules should never be condoned.

All action in the litigation should be considered in light of its implications under these rules. The drafting of a pleading is not just a necessary legal exercise to state a case or avoid a default— sometimes it is the only thing the arbiter reads until the litigation is well under way, and accordingly it shapes his or her important first impression of the case. The "speaking" pleading, in which the key facts and issues are recited sympathetically and at length, can be most useful if not overdone. The way in which one expresses a claim or defense may help decide the extent to which one may later be able to obtain discovery, or oppose requested discovery into one's own affairs, or obtain or oppose interim relief, or avoid joinder of a cause of action one would prefer to bring at another time or place, or have the issues tried by judge or jury. Decision on a preliminary injunctive application often is designed to preserve the "status quo." How one phrases that status can be quite important: Is the injunction, for example, sought to maintain existing employees' jobs while the case is pending? Or is it sought to maintain the aggrieved discharged employees' right to work? Language and form may not be determinative, but they can be most significant.

It is of course impossible for corporate counsel, who is assumed not to be a trained and experienced trial lawyer, to recognize all the procedural or even substantive implications incident to a single procedural step. This is the province of the trial attorney. But if the proper mutual relationship has been established, corporate counsel should be able to solicit the appropriate advice from trial counsel. All lawyers are, or should be, trained in how to inquire into new and different situations and explore new avenues. Working intimately with the trial attorney should be one of the more pleasant professional assignments of corporate counsel, and should prove helpful in developing the necessary expertise to build up his or her own internal trial capability if desired.

Some trial lawyers like to pretend that much of what they do is a kind of "second nature" or inherited or acquired expertise which really cannot be communicated to lay persons (including nontrial lawyers). Their responses to questions are couched in phrases such as: "This just isn't the kind of case in which summary judgment will succeed"; "A jury can't understand this type of a problem"; or "We never admit anything in a pleading." They may be right, but corporate counsel is entitled to some better explanation. He or she also is an attorney, and nothing should be so erudite as to be beyond the understanding of all but the trial attorney. Corporate counsel should ask "Why not?" Sometimes it will quickly appear that the trial attorney is simply employing the same technique of speaking with assurance and conviction which is so successful in court but hasn't yet thought through the logic. More frequently the reason for the recommendation is that the same kind of matter has always been handled that way. But times have changed, and a new, fresh look may reveal a better approach. If corporate counsel is to perform the management function properly, he or she must insist on trial counsel's explanation of any questioned areas, in terms that can be understood and evaluated. Corporate counsel must show trial counsel that he or she intends to remain firmly in command of policy matters. Ultimately, trial counsel's recommendation and expertise may be deferred to, but there is no excuse for doing so in ignorance. The corporate counsel who does might better have turned the whole matter over to the trial lawyer in the first place and then forgotten about it. He or she would thereby have saved the client a good deal of money and both attorneys a lot of time.

Interim Injunctions

The resolution of socioscientific disputes—and litigations generally —can take a very long time. As a result, sometimes the dispute is decided for practical purposes by early injunctive relief, such as by the temporary restraining order granted for very short periods until argument is possible; the temporary injunction, which lasts for a specified period of time; or the injunction *pendente lite,* which lasts for the duration of the litigation.

A corporate acquisition or merger may depend on present market conditions and will fail if final conclusion must await the outcome of a many-year litigation. The production and marketing of a drug may be predicated upon existing needs, which are expected to change. The building of a plant may be determined by construction costs, which in recent years have escalated so rapidly as to make many delayed projects uneconomic. In these kinds of cases, immediate attention must be focused on the urgent relief sought, even to the exclusion of longer-range litigation preparation if necessary. The latter can be dealt with if and when it becomes appropriate, but may have to be postponed simply because otherwise there will be no long range to look to.

All the other litigation considerations discussed elsewhere in this book are applicable here, only in a much more concentrated fashion. The single redeeming factor is that the other side will be under the same pressures. As so often in the socioscientific case, however, certain special aspects must be considered.

Credibility continues to be of prime importance and action should not be taken even in emergency which is inconsistent with true purpose and objective. The litigant who protests that a given course of action is physically or economically impossible—and then goes ahead and does it when compelled to by an injunction— cannot expect that much confidence will be reposed in later claims. The party who rushes pell-mell for preliminary equitable relief, clamoring that otherwise a business will be destroyed, but when refused such relief permits the main case to go along ploddingly, has disclosed true motivation and "game" tactics, at least if the adversary appreciates and chooses to emphasize the disparity. The adversary who defeats an injunctive request by demanding the posting of an expensive indemnity bond which cannot be furnished may well have lost the case if it later turns out that it must have known no such short-term stakes could possibly have been involved.

Emergency applications should not be used as a way to avoid work, a common practice with some who use the excuse of limited time to justify a request for dispensation with the normally required affidavits and memoranda. Instead, every effort should be made to appear with even *more* complete and persuasive papers to justify the emergency action requested or the opposition. Special care should be taken to avoid overreaching or overstatement upon which the arbiter may mistakenly rely in the rush to decide, and thereafter discover to have been in error. Otherwise the damage to credibility is unavoidable.

Corporate counsel should be particularly alert to the temporary restraining order or "TRO," which may otherwise be entered even before trial counsel has been retained. The TRO is often based on the application of only one party to the dispute, even before the formal pleadings have been served, allegedly because time is so critical that there is no opportunity for notice and argument. Typically it is to prevent some critical irreversible action, such as the destruction of a building a few hours later in violation of an alleged ownership interest and without previous notice.

The TRO is often used as a tactic, because even the brief delay is known to be of enormous importance to the other party. Sometimes, for example, a new environmental organization will claim very recent notice of major construction, destruction, or other activity. Generally, however, even though the particular organization involved may be a new one, its principals will have had previous notice. TROs rarely are sought in the absence of some previous notice of the dispute. Ordinarily the parties will have been negotiating or debating the differences and will have reached an impasse.

Corporate counsel must learn to recognize the kinds of cases in which the adversary is likely to use the TRO tactic, and anticipate it by retaining local trial counsel earlier than usual. A letter to the adversary requesting telephone notice of any TRO application, with the assurance of immediate response and appearance before the court (and with a copy to the court itself or the clerk if the conduct of the adversary is suspect) should at least cut off the *ex parte* aspect of the tactic. In important cases, advance preparation of affidavits and other responsive papers may be necessary as a precaution, even though they may never be used.

Motion Practice

The rule-of-reason approach calls for a minimum of pretrial motions. It sanctions only those for which there is a clear and substantial justification, which can be stated if necessary. This is quite different from the common practice of many trial attorneys and calls for explanation.

Motions, which are called by different names in different jurisdictions, are applications to a tribunal for some kind of action. There is substantially no limit to their nature and scope. They can be as sweeping as motions to dismiss or for summary judgment, which seek to terminate the litigation finally and conclusively, or as narrow as motions to separately state and number paragraphs of a complaint or to strike surplus language, which are often addressed only to the niceties of pleading legal causes of action.

The modern procedural rules adopted for the federal courts and in many other jurisdictions have generally liberalized the older strict practice. As a result, some of the more trivial pretrial motions are coming into disrepute at the trial bar. But many trial lawyers continue routinely to examine the pleadings and other conduct of an adversary and almost automatically make the appropriate routine motions as learned in law school or printed in a hornbook. The practice is so common and customary in some places that corporate counsel will not even be consulted or requested for authority.

The reasons for these motions are rarely stated. Frequently they are made mechanically, without a great deal of thought or consideration: "We always do it." When the matter has been turned over by the senior trial attorney to his or her junior in these circumstances the issue is foreclosed unless the junior seeks express authority to follow other than the standard practice. *Not* to make the routine motion, in fact, is therefore what requires analysis, so as to avoid subsequent criticism.

But there is another reason for these motions. It is to "teach the other side a lesson," "make them work," or "show them they've got a fight on their hands." Behind this in turn is the conviction that the adversary will "fold" if made to appreciate how much trouble and expense the litigation is going to entail. Sometimes this is because the motivation of the adversary is questioned and the litigation considered a "strike" suit. Where there is great inequality in financial resources or perceived commitment it may also be because the adversary's ability or willingness to bear the resulting large litigation costs is doubted.

Although the deliberate use of litigation procedure to harass seems clearly improper, apparently this kind of practice is not generally considered unethical. Some trial counsel will actually verbalize their intentions to "overwhelm the other side" and "make them pay through the nose for their case." The practice undoubtedly persists because it is sometimes successful, resulting in a litigation dropped or an advantageous settlement concluded. But this kind of occasional success is not justified in light of the enormous risks involved. The rule of reason demands a contrary approach.

The litigation impact would be disastrous were a memorandum describing such harassing tactics somehow to slip through and be discovered by the adversary, or were a disgruntled secretary or other employee, or even former staff attorney, to furnish such information. Corporate credibility would surely suffer and the outcome of the litigation would be seriously prejudiced, even if ethical propriety were sustained as a recognized part of the sporting approach. Direct evidence of this kind is rare, of course, but adversaries are not as stupid as sometimes painted and a pattern of technical motions can be presented as evidence of an intention to harass and obstruct. When the harassing party is a large corporation and the adversary a sympathetic local individual or so-called "consumer" or "public" representative, the jury or judge may punish, even if the bar will not, through the imposition of punitive damages.

I believe that this kind of perceived harassment and abuse of corporate financial power is in fact one of the two main reasons for the burgeoning punitive and exemplary damage judgments being assessed against corporate parties. The other is the corporation's change in its factual presentation *after* the dispute has gotten into the hands of its attorneys (discussed in Chapter 3), which similarly represents an effort to punish what is perceived as contrivance or fabrication by attorneys in pursuit of the sporting approach. In other words, corporations are not being punished for their underlying conduct, for which there is usually ample substantive punishment available by way of criminal prosecution or other separate punitive proceeding, but because of perceived use of what the public considers improper litigation tactics by attorneys who are presumptively authorized to speak and act on the corporation's behalf. What better reason to adopt the rule-of-reason approach?

A second reason for avoiding unjustified motions is expense. The trial attorney's assertion that "we'll make them work for their case" may be true enough, but it overlooks that the corporation will have to work just as hard and pay just as much—and probably a good deal harder and more. If the adversary is in fact poorly financed or carrying on a strike suit, the chances are good that it will do only a small fraction of the corporation's work, citing at most one or two cases, relying on the corporation's papers for research leads, and anticipating that the judge or the judge's law clerk will help. Spending ten thousand corporation dollars to beat down a claim realistically worth five thousand at most doesn't make a lot of sense unless there is some independent justification apart from the immediate dollars involved.

There is yet a third reason for establishing a presumption *against* the routine making of motions—they can be very bad litigation strategy. They educate the adversary in the defects of his or her case while corrective action is still possible. They compel the lazy opponent to do work and prepare a forceful case, and they encourage him or her to take action in the client's best interest which otherwise might have been overlooked or avoided because of a contingent-fee relationship.

Motion practice has been refined to its present state as a means of assisting the parties to prepare their cases for hearing and trial. It is very much a way of balancing some of the inequities in the system as between parties of unequal resource. Ordinarily the smaller, weaker, less well-financed litigant benefits more by seeking a tribunal's assistance. His or her adversary is better equipped both to prepare for the many alternatives without assistance of the tribunal and independently to finance the broader research and investigations required.

Consider, for example, a motion to dismiss a litigation for failure to allege an essential element of the cause of action, such as notice to the corporation of the defect which caused the injury. This is a substantial motion, not a trivial or dilatory one, designed to win the case and not to obstruct or harass. *If* the law is clear and certain that notice is essential and not subject to interpretation or change, and *if* the facts are equally clear and certain that notice was not given, again not subject to interpretation or fabrication or distortion, the motion will dispose of the case finally and completely and should be made.

But neither law nor fact is usually that clear. The doctrine of strict liability, where notice may not be required, is expanding almost every day, with courts sometimes almost legislating new rules. In the large corporation, with thousands of employees acting and speaking for it all over the world, it is difficult to be certain of anything. If there is any significant doubt in these legal or factual respects, or any other, why educate the opponent that notice is required? Why suggest that he or she research the developing strict liability theory? Why pinpoint the key factual issues towards which he or she must direct depositions of corporate personnel and witnesses, demands for documents, interrogatories, the general investigation, and other discovery? The tribunal will almost certainly give the adversary permission to amend a pleading if somehow the case can be brought within a strict liability concept, or allow him or her to initiate or to complete discovery into relevant areas before any final decision on the motion. Ordinarily it is far better strategy to withhold fire if there is doubt on any of these issues. The application can then be made at some later point when the opportunities for amendment and discovery are more limited. Indeed, if pretrial procedures permit, and they often do, the application can be made at the hearing or trial *after* the adversary has rested his or her case. Then the opportunity for change of theory and discovery and presentation of other evidence is substantially gone and victory will indeed be final.

Why make a motion for partial summary judgment, seeking to dismiss only one of several causes of action, even if one is categorically certain of the result? It doesn't save preparation, for if one *really* is certain, no further preparation is needed (and if one isn't certain, the motion ordinarily shouldn't be made, as above). Conceivably there is some advantage to early education of the arbiter, but the arbiter who decides the motion may not be the arbiter who finally tries the case. It may be that the application made at the trial will have the preferable effect, by casting doubt on the remainder of the adversary's factual presentations as well as on his or her legal theories.

This is not to suggest that there may not be sound reasons for motions to dismiss, even when there is doubt, or motions for partial summary judgment. On occasion it may be worth the risk in order to compel an adversary to evaluate his or her position more realistically and thereby enhance settlement possibilities, or to begin education of the arbiter so that he or she will understand the complexities and nuances of the litigation.

The governing principle is that there must be a sound reason for making any application. That reason must be able to withstand public disclosure, if necessary, and not be for harassment, obstruction, or delay. It must outweigh the disadvantages of making the application, including expense. Simply stated, this is a presumption *against* making motions in rule-of-reason cases.

Should it be necessary to make a strictly technical or dilatory motion, which an adversary or others might perceive as part of an effort to harass, it is usually wise voluntarily to explain fully the reason for the motion. A motion to strike scandalous language in a pleading, for example, can be explained as necessary to avoid the adversary repeating it in other connections during the litigation or elsewhere. Even a motion to dismiss based on a statute of limitations or statute of frauds defense might include brief reference to the standard public policy considerations that have led legislatures to adopt laws of this kind, which sometimes appear inequitable or unfair to laypersons.

Emphasis upon the negative, upon *not* making motions, has been necessary in this section because the practice is so commonly to the contrary. However, the value of sound and constructive motions can be great and they should never be overlooked in exploring the weapons in the litigation arsenal. Rule of reason socio-scientific litigations call for new and different motions, specifically designed to apply to the new and different kinds of cases which are emerging. Do not let trial counsel inexperienced in these kinds of matters reject an apparently sensible suggestion with "We never make that kind of motion." With limited exceptions, tribunals will consider substantially any reasonable application the mind can dream up; the limits are only one's imagination. Sometimes a motion seeking disclosure may even be appropriate largely to demonstrate the adversary's recalcitrance and automatic opposition, and unwillingness to participate in the give-and-take of the rule of reason approach. Motion practice in the socioscientific litigation should in fact provide one of the most intriguing challenges to corporate as well as to litigation expertise. The pure creative thinking it demands is one key to success in all litigation, as it is to so much else in life.

Corporate staff counsel who wishes to do so should participate actively in oral argument and advocacy of motions. Where a legal principle is involved, he or she may well be one of the outstanding experts in the field. Often he or she will have detailed knowledge of the facts as well. Such an intimate participatory relationship between corporate and trial counsel in pretrial motion practice provides another opportunity for rewarding and pleasant professional exchange.

Discovery

In pretrial discovery, like motion practice, trial counsel too frequently furnishes automatic responses and takes almost mechanical action: "We *always* serve an oral deposition notice with our complaint"; "We *always* want to see the documents before conducting examinations"; "We *always* ask for our discovery first."

Although considerable discovery in the major socioscientific litigation is usually necessary, the same presumption should apply: Discovery should only be conducted for some substantial reason *other* than harassment or obstruction, and the reason must outweigh probable disadvantages, including litigation costs.

The reasons for the presumption are very much the same as those regarding pretrial motions, although perhaps not as obvious because the move to discovery is so standard and routine. Trial counsel will sometimes treat a question regarding the desirability of suggested discovery with disbelief and as not worthy of serious consideration. Yet the benefits in *not* conducting certain kinds of discovery can be even greater than for motions.

In the major socioscientific litigation, so commonly initiated by a "public interest" group, for example, an effort will sometimes be made by trial counsel to discover the identities of all the members of the group, or to find out who is financing the litigation, or how much adversary counsel is being paid. Sometimes this kind of inquiry into standing and motivation is justified. But far more often it reflects an antagonism and desire for retribution suggestive of the way in which the public perceived the General Motors investigation of Ralph Nader. It involves a risk which should be assumed only after the most careful consideration.

The expense of discovery is undoubtedly the largest single element in total litigation cost. Even though the costs of all components of litigation are great, motion practice and trial can pale by comparison. There are only so many hours to a day and so many people needed in a courtroom and for support, so that even lengthy trials have finite limits. But there is no such limit to discovery. In one case in which I was involved, for example, six depositions were running concurrently, one in northern Ireland, one in England, two in New York, two at other points in the United States. Over two thousand depositions were noticed in another; more than fifty paralegals were involved in discovery in a third. Documents to be examined, selected, indexed, digested, and copied frequently run into the tens of millions of pages.

A motion can often be copied in major part from an earlier similar motion, for which the needed research was completed and needs only to be brought up to date. But there is very little one can do to cut down the time required to examine a document, or to travel to a deposition and ask the questions, one by one, of each new witness. All of this may be more than justified by the information developed. But clearly one should not assume such a burden without an affirmative decision that the costs are warranted.

Even more than motion practice, discovery is designed to help the weaker party and that is usually (although not always) its effect. The litigant with greater resources can hire investigators, who can be quite expensive; it can conduct interviews and document searches of friendly and public sources, using liberal freedom of information acts for the latter; it can undertake research; and it can otherwise buy and pay for what is needed far more readily than the weaker adversary. This is especially true of the socioscientific type of case, where so much of the final decision turns upon public attitudes that can be discovered without court assistance. Given a real choice as counsel for a corporate party to a major socioscientific case, I would ordinarily opt for no judicial discovery rather than mutual discovery.

Such a choice is rarely offered expressly, of course, but the issue is not academic. A litigation will frequently present opportunities for limiting or even excluding discovery, if only the policy is clear and the opportunities are recognized and seized. Where a motion for a preliminary injunction is sought against a company, for example, a common part of opposition will be to emphasize the controverted facts and the need for discovery before such drastic relief is entered. In a case where the company itself has most of the facts, and clearly needs much less discovery than the opposition, it may be far better to seize upon the assertions of urgency and inadequate funding by offering to go to trial on the whole case, promptly. The adversary may be hard put to reject the offer even though it appreciates how much it needs discovery, its bluff having been unexpectedly but effectively called; or it may be forced to compress its requirements into an extremely tight and unsatisfactory timetable. Moreover, even if the offer is rejected, most tribunals today have the power needed to advance the hearing on the merits of the full case to the hearing on the request for a preliminary injunction and join the two. Certainly the company also will be going to final trial before it is as well prepared as it would like; but it should be much better able to do so than the opposition. If so, the risks of no discovery are amply justified.

Similar opportunities for limiting discovery may be presented whenever an adversary pleads a special need for early relief, or charges delaying tactics, or claims to be impoverished or otherwise unable to bear mounting litigation costs. But taking the action needed to obtain such a limitation requires that there have been a previous decision, in which corporate counsel has joined, that limitation is desirable if mutually imposed.

Discovery does limit risk, of course, by furnishing access to the opposition's facts and arguments. The need for the most incisive perception of the adversary case has already been pointed out. Many trial counsel will be quite reluctant to cut off discovery because of the possibility that something will have been overlooked or some step will be taken which turns out to have been a mistake. Their recommendations against such a course, however, may themselves overlook the other side of the coin—the risks that discovery itself creates. Their perceptions of the matter quite naturally emphasize the need to avoid mistake and error as even more crucial than winning: Loss to an adversary with a good case cannot be seriously criticized; loss because of one's own error can be.

Litigation is made up of all kinds of risks, however, and the risks of not conducting discovery may be outweighed by the risks of furnishing such discovery to the adversary. Here again, therefore, corporate counsel should take firm control after evaluating all the information and recommendations. He or she should assure trial counsel that any decision to forgo discovery will be the client's and that no "second guessing" will result if it turns out to have been wrong.

We turn now to a consideration of the specific methods of discovery generally available. Procedures of course vary by jurisdiction and even with kinds of cases, but many of the problems are common ones.

One question generally posed with regard to all discovery is: Which comes first? Does one seek documents first in order to know what kinds of questions to ask in a deposition? Does one seek the deposition first so as to know what documents to ask for? Does one try to beat the other side to discovery, so as to be able to limit flexibility and opportunity for molding and shaping contentions to meet what is discovered? Or does one seek to let the other side go first for the educational benefit of being able thereafter to proceed more effectively with one's own discovery or so that the opposition's questions will be based upon the most limited knowledge?

There are no absolute or categorical answers to any of these questions, although trial lawyers very often follow certain standard procedures in each case. Such a standardized course may be acceptable and even necessary in the routine insurance-company type of negligence practice, where the form demand for a bill of particulars must go out with the pleading to order to limit cost. But they are not appropriate to major socioscientific cases. Trial attorneys inexperienced in such cases should be urged to review these kinds of routine practices in light of the special facts and issues presented.

Analysis of the case almost always will furnish a reasonably clear answer to these questions. The really significant information will be known only to a few key persons, in which event their oral depositions must precede any other intelligent discovery. Or the documentary record will be crucial, with some danger of loss or destruction of documents, in which case these must be obtained first and preserved. Or one's own employees may refuse to take the case seriously and subjecting them first to adversary examination will appear to pose no serious problem, in which case such a course will make it possible thereafter to obtain the fuller cooperation and authority needed to prepare properly. These are not usually very difficult decisions. Unfortunately, they are made too infrequently.

Opposition to requested discovery constitutes another general concern, especially applicable to rule-of-reason cases. Such opposition, if overruled, may be made to appear obstructive; if sustained, it may be argued to evidence fear of what would have been produced. Accordingly, it is important to have in mind substantial reasons for seeking to limit discovery by an opponent, and where appropriate to express such reasons in the opposition itself.

Oral Depositions

Except for the need to avoid harassment and obstruction, rule-of-reason depositions are similar to depositions generally. They fall into two general categories: "discovery" depositions, where the objective is to find something out or pin something down, and depositions preserving testimony because the witness is expected to die or is leaving the jurisdiction or may for some other reason be unavailable when needed, where the objective is to preserve the testimony in proper form for use later at a hearing or trial. Usually any single deposition will contain elements falling into both categories. One's own chief executive, for example, may be interrogated by the adversary for purposes of exploring knowledge of the corporation's conduct, but advanced age or planned retirement may also make the probability of the executive testifying years later questionable.

In the strict adversary discovery deposition, the examiner's objective is to find out everything he or she can about the case. The examiner should accordingly be thoroughly prepared, with a careful, written outline of all the matters to be explored, including the existence and location of documents. The examiner should have on hand any relevant documents that are available for use in refreshing recollection and in suggesting further lines of inquiry. The more the witness can be made to say the better; even apparently irrelevant comments may furnish clues to a witness's personality and weaknesses for later use in trial cross-examination. If he or she answers a question, "What time did the conference take place?" by furnishing all the details as to place, attendees, and what was said and by whom, in theory so much the better. Of course, there are limits. Even though the adversary may not be able to use the deposition at trial unless the witness is seriously ill or unavailable for reasons beyond the adversary's control, the transcript may be important to a motion or in connection with some other aspects of the dispute. And of course the witness *may* die or leave the adversary employ and go to Brazil. Appropriate motions to strike as nonresponsive or other procedural moves may prove necessary in an effort to ensure that the otherwise inadmissible statements do not somehow get into the final hearing record. (I can not promise much success for such efforts, however. Where the witness is really unavailable, these kinds of things have a way of getting into evidence one way or another, like it or not.)

The above reference to the examiner's purpose in conducting a deposition, usually trial counsel's assignment, is significant in pointing up how corporate counsel must approach the discovery depositions of his or her own corporate employees. In this, of course, he or she plays a very active role. With very limited exceptions, corporate counsel must make them understand that such depositions can only function negatively; they can move the corporation's case in just one direction—backwards. It would be best if the adversary did not have access to the company witness at all. Substantially anything the witness says can be used against him or her; unless he or she dies or leaves the company, it cannot be used affirmatively. It is surprising how few trial counsel recognize this. Some will suggest that corporate counsel round up all the company's best witnesses and have them testify, one after the other: "We'll show them."

Of course, on occasion, "showing them" on discovery depositions may be justified. It may be conducive to settlement; it may be a way of getting one's story through an obstreperous adversary counsel and to his or her client; it may be useful as evidence on subsequent applications to the tribunal. But in the absence of some such special reason, the best course is to respond to whatever proper demands the adversary makes, produce the witnesses identified or requested, and let them answer as responsively but as briefly as they can. Any other company personnel to whom they voluntarily refer for support will promptly become successor witnesses; any files to which they voluntarily refer will become search candidates. The rule-of-reason approach calls only for elimination of the sporting and the game approaches to litigation. It does not reject the adversary approach or purport to do the adversary's job. Indeed, properly viewed, the rule of reason is the most effective adversary litigation weapon of all because it is calculated to maximize the chances for litigation success. It is perfectly consistent, therefore, to advise that the fewer leads and less information one's own company witnesses unnecessarily furnish the opponent, the better.

It is worth repeating that corporate counsel should have worked with his or her company witnesses from the inception of the dispute and should continue to participate actively in their preparation for deposition. He or she should of course point out the reasons for limiting their responses and indicate that the approach will probably be quite different at the hearing (to be discussed in Chapter 7). Witness understanding is essential to effective testimony.

Does one "cross-examine" one's own employee witnesses on a discovery deposition conducted by the adversary? Ordinarily not. But if there is some realistic possibility that the evidence to be adduced will be unavailable at the hearing, either through that witness, some other witness, or documents, or that the information is so crucial that failure to disclose could reasonably be viewed by the arbiter as disingenuous or worse, or some other substantial purpose (such as settlement) is to be served, then the information should be developed.

Does one object while one's own company witnesses are being examined on discovery deposition? Technically, most such objections are usually unnecessary. In most jurisdictions, objections of substance, such as those based on hearsay and relevance, for example, are automatically preserved until the hearing; objections to form, such as to the leading nature of a question, must be made to be preserved, but these are usually quite unimportant when an adversary is examining. After all, even though technically the adversary may be conducting a "direct" examination and therefore be prohibited from "leading" the witness, what realistic possibility is there that he or she can "lead" an adverse company president down the garden path to a desired answer? Indeed, in some jurisdictions "leading" is permitted when an adversary is being questioned.

On the other hand, some objections may be essential, with the witness even instructed to refuse to answer. Questions designed to elicit information falling within attorney-client privilege or to discover business secrets clearly fall within this category. Sometimes a seemingly interminable examination must be attacked on the grounds of irrelevance and harassment—or the employee will never get back to work.

What about the objection designed to give the witness time to reflect; or the "speaking" objection, which includes within its statement a suggestion the witness might consider in shaping an answer and might otherwise overlook; or the objection designed to take adversary heat off the witness and deflect it to his or her attorney, so that the witness will be calmer and better able to think? It is the job of counsel to protect the witness from the improper conduct of an adversary attorney. Yet it is *not* proper for counsel to interfere with an opponent's reasonable opportunities for developing hostile information—indeed, the discovery deposition process is specifically designed to afford this chance.

Recognizing proper versus improper adversary conduct is not easy, especially for the trial advocate personally engaged in the adversary fray. Some element of doubt and suspicion in a series of rapid, tight, cross-examination questions may well be justified; use of epithets may not. The best one can say is that a delicate balancing of litigation judgment is required to know how to protect without overstepping reasonable bounds. Corporate counsel can be of substantial assistance to trial counsel by attending the important depositions and furnishing the perspective of an informed onlooker as to how things may later be perceived by a judge or jury.

Does one seek in effect to "cross-examine" an adversary witness during a discovery deposition, even though technically conducting a direct examination? Again, yes and no. Suppose the witness has testified to a conversation and one possesses a document directly contradicting this testimony. The purpose of the deposition is to discover information and positions, and if the witness clearly has no answer except to retract stated testimony, why not save the document until trial when the witness can be exposed before the jury, without having had long months or years to develop the excuse that he or she wasn't feeling well, or that the stenographic reporter misunderstood, or that the questions were too heated and answered too quickly? On the other hand, there *may* be an explanation and one should know it before relying too heavily on the document. Or the document may be later produced during document discovery, and it would be better to get the response pinned down now before the witness and opposing attorney have too much time to think about it. Or the "cross-examination" may be useful for settlement or other pretrial litigation purpose. Or failure to disclose might somehow be made to appear as a shabby or improper tactic. Fortunately there is usually adequate time during a deposition to consider the conflicting considerations involved in these kinds of problem. Once again, corporate counsel can be of much assistance in furnishing friendly independent advice as to where the balance of conflicting considerations should be set.

The good trial attorney will also continually keep in mind how the written record will look, especially during an oral deposition where the pauses or intonations or red faces will not appear (unless the attorney personally notes them on the record). This is also a most difficult assignment and participating corporate counsel can be helpful in this respect as well.

Corporate counsel's deposition and other active participation not only should be of substantial help to trial counsel, but should enable corporate counsel to make sound judgments about the quality of the selected trial attorney: Does he or she understand and consider the strategy and tactic issues? Watch the record? Repeat critical questions which the witness seeks to evade, so as to get the key questions and answers in juxtaposition for later use on motion or at trial? Does he or she construct questions carefully, so as to be short, simple, and sweet, leaving no room for escape or maneuvering out of reach? Does he or she tie up loose ends with "Have you exhausted your recollection?" and "Is there anything else?" Self-doubting corporate counsel who participate once will quickly appreciate how easy it is for them to distinguish between the alert, careful, and diligent trial attorney, and the plodding or pedestrian. This is corporate counsel's job. There is rarely a good excuse for discovering the inadequacies of trial counsel only at the time of trial or after a disastrous verdict. Reliance upon a simple license to practice law and alleged experience and expertise cannot be condoned in the face of the conceded inadequacy of so much of the trial bar, the statistical guarantee that there will be problems when dealing with a large enough number of matters and individuals, and the uniqueness and novelty of rule-of-reason socioscientific cases.

Written Interrogatories

Written questions addressed to a party or witness can be a good substitute for, or supplement to, oral depositions. The responses are usually prepared by adversary counsel, however, so they will rarely be as spontaneous or as likely to disclose gaps, defects, or materials of use on cross-examination. On the other hand, they can also be a quick and efficient way of getting to the heart of a matter and pinpointing the issues or areas calling for other kinds of discovery. Where both parties are applying the rule of reason, written depositions may reduce delay and expense by orders of magnitude.

Corporate counsel should ordinarily undertake to prepare at least the first draft of response to adversary written interrogatories, although this will not be possible where trial counsel has conducted all the investigation and other preparation. The answers should be responsive and not obviously evasive or excessively self-serving. Motions to strike or limit improper interrogatories are in order; but use of obstructive tactics may well backfire when later presented to judge or jury.

Documents

Although general rules are questionable, especially with regard to litigation of the major socioscientific case, it is probably safe to say that document discovery is usually the single most important discovery weapon. One picture may indeed be worth a thousand words. Most good trial lawyers understand this and corporate counsel need only be sure they explore all the appropriate avenues —by document demand, by written interrogatory, by oral deposition questions regarding files, at pretrial conference, and whenever or wherever else search is justified. Excessive document requests may be burdensome, but when in doubt the cost of inspection is usually well worthwhile.

As already discussed, it should be corporate counsel's primary responsibility to manage the document search within his or her own company, a step preferably initiated even before trial counsel is retained. Indeed, corporate counsel's litigation education program, including an explanation to company personnel of the significance and dangers of ill-considered documents, should have preceded the dispute itself so that the documents produced will pose a minimum of problems. But he or she should use the document discovery process as an integral part of the ongoing training program. This is as much true of the oral deposition as of the document aspects, but company deponents rarely have to be told much after they have gone through the unpleasant personal experience of an intense deposition grilling. Document discovery, on the other hand, infrequently represents the same personal involvement.

Company directors will listen politely when counsel cautions that discretion be employed in keeping notes of board meetings and personal diaries. But nothing is quite so effective as a good "for instance." Production of a personal diary page expressing an inadequately considered opinion or understanding can sometimes have such a valuable cathartic effect as in fact to be worth even its damaging impact on the litigation.

What about the common litigation tactic of "overwhelming" the opposition by producing staggering numbers of documents, sometimes not even requested, or deliberately shuffled and mixed up. I regard this not only as inconsistent with the rule-of-reason approach but as dangerous. If perceived and uncovered by the adversary, it contradicts the corporation's assertion of openness and integrity. In addition, unevaluated materials are likely to get through, for which one will later be unprepared. The strategy calling for maximum obtaining of documents naturally has its obverse, suggesting minimum disclosure. In one situation, however, an aspect of this tactic may be appropriate. If the adversary is demanding documents known to be privileged so that the judge will read them, it may be well to construe his or her requests broadly and furnish large volumes of privileged documents in the hope that the judge will rule generally on groups or categories of documents rather than trouble to read so many obviously privileged pages.

Company counsel in the multinational corporation must also remain alert to the foreign document problem. Courts in this country are increasingly inclined to compel production of documents located abroad in the custody of divisions, subsidiaries, or even affiliates over which a litigant has control. This request may sometimes cause considerable embarrassment in foreign jurisdictions whose mores and laws are different from our own. Disclosures of payments made to foreign officials, termed "bribery" but often standard practice in the countries involved, have even toppled governments (albeit to be replaced by others equally corrupt). Sometimes a production order may bring the litigant into conflict with equally mandatory secrecy statutes of foreign states, as has been the case with certain Swiss and Lichtenstein bank disclosures and with document orders relating to international oil companies' relationships with Middle East government officials. These can pose the most serious commercial and legal problems. Advance planning of the structure of document control and of the kinds of documents prepared can do much to help. But there will be no simple answers, and corporate counsel's continued and informed participation will be essential throughout.

One final matter of importance: the extremely damaging document, with respect to which there is no adequate response. Necessarily this means that the company's case is a bad one—otherwise there would be some answer, such as mistake, stupidity, lack of authority and the like. As in the case where no affirmative presentation can be developed, the rule of reason mandates that the litigation be terminated as quickly and cheaply as possible, preferably before the adversary discovers the damaging evidence. (The same principle applies to oral testimony, although the problem is rarely as well defined or obvious.) Only a miscarriage of justice can save the day, and this certainly is not the objective of the rule of reason or any other sound system of dispute resolution.

Even if the document seems reasonably safe from disclosure, either because the adversary hasn't made the proper discovery requests or the document appears somehow exempt from production, termination is essential. These facts may allow more time to work out a satisfactory resolution of the case, but should not be relied on as security when the issues are serious ones. Corporate credibility, responsibility, and integrity are at stake. The risks of inadvertent or improper disclosure, or blackmail, are too great to accept. Corporate credibility demands doing the right thing, always, and when you discover you are wrong, the right thing to do is to admit it and proceed by seeking the most equitable settlement for the company which is consistent with the facts. If company personnel are themselves to believe that the company means what it says, even its internal conduct must be consistent. Company executives, scientists, technicians, and all others involved in the process are not trial advocates capable of moving from one posture to another. They can only proclaim integrity candidly and convincingly if they mean it.

Other Discovery

There is little limit except imagination to the other kinds of discovery available in the modern tribunal, much as with motion practice generally. Requests for admissions, inspections, and medical examinations are among the most common, but only because they are designed to meet the most common requirements of the traditional cases. Because socioscientific cases are somewhat different, new discovery measures may well be needed to accommodate them. Jointly conducted or supervised research, using qualified independent experts and agreed-upon protocols, may be desirable in order to investigate new questions without wasting scarce laboratory facilities and limited talents. Agreed-upon public, industry, or group surveys may be needed to explore relevant sociological or economic developments or opinions, public attitudes, or business practices, at a minimum of interference with the rights and interests of third parties not involved directly in the dispute. Unfortunately, administrative and judicial tribunals have been slow to accommodate themselves to the new litigations, and these kinds of discovery are rarely ordered in an adversary context in the absence of agreement of the parties. But the time is surely coming, and corporate counsel who encourage the process will be serving not only their corporations, but society in general as well.

The Prehearing Conference

Although some tribunals are conducting prehearing conferences in steps, the first coming relatively early in a litigation, quite commonly the prehearing or pretrial conference is what its name implies—pretty much the final step in the pretrial process, before the hearing actually begins. At this point the hearing arbiter will participate in the case to see to it that the hearing is conducted as efficiently and expeditiously as possible. Witness lists will be exchanged, exhibits marked for identification, issues defined, and other action taken to limit the hearing as much as possible to the presentation of evidence and related argument.

The prehearing conference is not, however, the last step before hearing. It is in fact the beginning of the hearing itself (unless the same arbiter has previously been involved in motions or other pretrial proceedings) and should be dealt with accordingly. There is no dividing line in a judge's mind between what is heard from a litigant at the opening of a pretrial conference and what the same litigant may say in a formal opening at the hearing itself. The two must be consistent or credibility suffers. If one is properly prepared for pretrial, as one should be, the opportunity can be used for presenting the case in summary or highlight, gaining advantage over an unprepared adversary, creating the best first impression (which is most important), and achieving the benefit of repetition when the same consistent presentation is repeated in detail at the hearing.

Adequate advance preparation for the prehearing conference makes it possible also to seize otherwise unavailable opportunities. The adversary may be persuaded to waive jury trial (if that is an objective) through recitation of the great burdens it will involve and persuasion of the court that the opponent's early trial request should be permitted only if the trial is a nonjury one. Adequate demand for privileged materials the adversary may intend to use at the hearing will obtain them in advance, or pinpoint adversary disingenuity in withholding what he or she should have known was later to be used. The varied possibilities make it essential that corporate counsel participate actively with trial counsel in the development of the strategy and, where possible, attend the event as well.

Joint Preparation

The major socioscientific case is very commonly a "big" case, involving a number of parties. Usually they will be aligned on one side or the other for convenience of the tribunal, but in fact their interests may vary considerably. It may be essential for those aligned together in interest to work together in preparation to save expense and avoid getting in each other's way (being "whipsawed"), but they should no more "let their hair down" with each other than with an adversary or the arbiter. Even if the law seems to protect privilege or work product when counsel for different parties work on a common defense, caution is required in making disclosures. Effort should be made to seek special added protections, such as by stipulation or court application, where such disclosure is necessary.

It is essential that trial counsel and his or her associates maintain their litigation presences at all times, in and out of court, in the country club and at the bar convention as well as before the jury. Never show glee at a point won; it was won because it should have been won, not because of a clever lawyer's argument. Never snicker at testimony; the arbiter alone decides whether the witness is telling the truth and doesn't relish the adversary's assumption of that function. Maintain the proper "poker" face throughout; always be "selling" in the proper sense of advocating a client's just position. These truisms are as valid in joint preparation as in adversary appearance.

How then does one work with co-litigation counsel representing another party? This is a most difficult assignment, requiring all the sensitivity and judgment a trial lawyer can muster. He or she must—without special power—be able to persuade *other* trial counsel, individuals who have trial lawyers' egos and represent interests that may be adversary in some respects. He or she can not show them up to their own clients nor appear to be directing the show, yet at the same time must orchestrate the performance.

The answer again calls for the most intimate relationship between corporate and trial counsel. Trial counsel must feel free to confidently proceed without concern for his or her own client standing, and must be able to do the work for co-litigation counsel, yet let them take the credit for it with their own clients, the arbiter, and all others. The pressures of their other business and the opportunities for them to save time and money may well make it possible for one to in effect control the litigation, in much the same fashion as by voluntarily assuming tribunal and adversary litigation burdens. But in this case counsel must also surrender personal ego considerations, so that co-litigation counsel will trust and accept his or her actions without jealousy or antagonism.

This is a large assignment to fill, particularly where the litigation expense is great. But it can be the best way. It is the outcome of the litigation that counts, not which party appears to be responsible for success or which trial lawyer is the most brilliant. And while the other parties may be spending less, it need not increase litigation expense excessively for the corporate client, especially since it intends to prepare thoroughly in any event. If trial and corporate counsel mutually understand what they are doing, their own success should be satisfaction enough to them and their client. And if the matter is handled as it should be, quite probably the other parties will recognize ultimately where credit actually is due.

Hearings, Trials, and Appeals

Chapter 7

Many attorneys treat hearings, trials, and appeals as somehow very different from everything that has gone before. They approach them with fear and trepidation, sometimes building themselves up into a frenzy of emotional tension. They will do almost anything to delay or avoid. This attitude is one important explanation for the much-too-common settlement "on the courthouse steps."

It should already be clear that the hearing or trial, and even more so, the subsequent appeal, are in fact not separate or isolated events at all, but only the tips of the litigation iceberg. In the major socioscientific case, their costs, however large, are small parts of the total. Their outcome is for the most part predetermined by pretrial and of course by the underlying facts. They should reflect both the record of the facts (which should themselves have been influenced by corporate counsel's educational efforts) and the record developed by counsel from the inception of the dispute, including the "self-serving" documents and the education of the arbiter initiated at the first appearance before him or her. If all of these have been well handled, there are no great surprises left and the formal appearance itself can be welcomed and relished.

Why then are even well-prepared and important socioscientific litigations so often settled on the eve of trial, when the work has been completed and all that remains is the final presentation? In the smaller, strictly private dispute, this may be because the parties haven't adequately prepared or evaluated their claims, or haven't really gotten together or given much thought to the matter until a judge begins to apply pressure. But this should not be true of the major public-interest case. If litigation preparation has been handled properly, nothing very startling should mark its conclusion.

The most common reason for pretrial settlement is unjustified fear: Corporate counsel fears the risks of the unknown; trial counsel fears not measuring up to client expectations, and the consequent criticism and impairment of reputation. These two fears combine synergistically to induce a settlement that may not be in the client's best interest, for the settlement reflects an effort to minimize the *attorneys'* risks, not the client's. If the cost of litigation is considered as one factor in the evaluation of a case, as it must be, it follows by simple logic that in the absence of some adverse development, a litigant's settlement terms should harden as the case proceeds. If one has already paid the three hundred thousand dollars of litigation expense pretrial was assumed to cost and the case has gotten no worse, why settle at the end for a figure no more advantageous than that rejected at the inception?

"Courthouse step" settlements should be accepted only if equal to earlier acceptable settlement terms, revised to compensate both for litigation burden and expense *and* any modified evaluation which proper pretrial preparation has developed. The well-prepared litigant has already borne the major expense and assumed the unknown risks—he or she should reap the benefits of this labor and investment by proceeding to trial.

This philosophy, not a common one, will require corporate counsel's authorization and sometimes insistence. If continuing, formal evaluations of the case, including its litigation costs, have been maintained as suggested in Chapter 4 the logic will be hard to challenge. If the proper relationship between corporate and trial counsel has been fostered, the trial attorney will have the confidence required to proceed.

The Dramatic Presentation

A trial or hearing, and an appeal, are dramatic presentations intended to convince a unique audience—the arbiter. Unlike other dramatic presentations, there is usually only one performance on which everything depends and, despite the best preparation, there are some inevitable uncertainties to the adversary's evidence and even as to how one's own witnesses will act and react. The performance accordingly demands the litigation equivalent of even more rehearsals and alternative scripts than a play.

Freedom to reflect on dealing with the unknown and uncertain requires that preparation for the known and certain be so thorough as to demand little additional thought. A trial memorandum (really a book or series of volumes), containing an analysis of every anticipated point of law, each in a form that can be quickly revised to suit the need of the moment, should be available to hand up to the arbiter on short notice. The trial memorandum should also contain a digest, in easy-to-follow form, of the direct and cross-examination testimony of each witness for each party, keyed to exhibits and with indications of when each exhibit is to be offered in evidence and for what purpose. The jury questions ("voir dire"), the opening, at least an outline of the summation, drafts of motions in as final a form as possible, indexes to facts, document controls, and all other litigation aids should be included in whatever form is best suited to the particular case and the trial attorney's own experience.

Trial practice demands that the trial lawyer be able to respond immediately and effectively to the unexpected. One secret to good practice is to reduce that unexpected to the absolute minimum through advance preparation. Perhaps only 5 percent or less of the preparation will be used, but the balance is necessary and economically justified because the identity of that precise 5 percent cannot be predetermined. Mistake or misjudgment may be excusable in the heat of battle over an order to show cause when there was no notice, but there is no excuse for failure to prepare for an event that should have been anticipated. By preparing for all reasonable contingencies, one is better prepared for the unknown.

There are economic limits to preparation, of course. Cost must be balanced against resulting risk, another area in which effective interchange between corporate and trial counsel is needed. Such decisions are not the responsibility of either attorney alone.

Like any other dramatic production, the presentation should start slowly, build up to a peak, and reflect throughout the desired attitudes of courtesy, respect, and firmness. The evidence should be planned so as to intersperse excitement with routine, with breaks in pattern, changes of pace, and even comic and other planned relief from ennui. None of this can be artificial, contrived, or otherwise suggestive of distortion.

Two general trial aspects of the major socioscientific litigation deserve special emphasis: the need to maintain a proper litigation presence throughout, and the need to build up arbiter and jury confidence gradually.

As to presence: Judges, juries, and other arbiters have usually had some exposure to our litigation system and even to its "sporting" aspects. They understand that trial attorneys are advocates, retained to advance a point of view not necessarily in accord with their own, and that they will sometimes employ "tricks" in the effort to succeed. Frequently trial arbiters consider it their assignment to watch for what the attorney *really* believes, assuming (usually quite incorrectly) that his or her intimate knowledge of the case affords complete insights, and for the tricks which might obfuscate or mislead. Their perceptions are, of course, subject to distortion and they may view an innocent smile, side-glance, or joking remark as of great significance, and an honest mistake in citation or reference as a "trick." The same litigation presence required from the beginning, even in dealings with co-litigation counsel, is required in the courtroom as well. The administration of justice is a serious business and any party who treats it in any other fashion will hurt his or her case. Even if the game approach is acceptable to attorneys, it is not to laypersons, and untoward expressions of pleasure or disappointment at winning and losing "points" are unacceptable. Badgering or browbeating a witness, and disrespect to an arbiter or colleague are similarly improper as evidencing abuse of the process. It is essential that the trial attorney, and each person in the hearing room identified as an associate (including client and witnesses), constantly consider how every action, every statement, and even manner of dress appear to the jury and arbiter. I have seen a small American flag button worn by an attorney antagonize a juror, who considered it a sign that the client adhered to an unacceptable reactionary viewpoint.

As to confidence: Because there is such doubt regarding the integrity of the litigation process, when possible trial counsel should try to start quietly and slowly, gradually building up the understanding and confidence with the tribunal which make an aggressive attack eventually acceptable. The arbiter or jury has not been exposed to the years of pretrial; they begin with the parties on an equal footing. The trial attorney who from the beginning shouts and derides is considered to be simply one who shouts and derides; the trial attorney who waits until he or she has earned the right to this kind of attack by virtue of carefully presented evidence achieves his or her point.

The following sections discuss the several aspects of the hearing and appeals processes, once again roughly in the order in which they occur and without any suggestion of an underlying theme. Even though these processes constitute the primary province of the trial lawyer, corporate counsel's active involvement is a significant aspect of his or her litigation management function. In addition, personal participation in at least one major trial should be an important part of every corporate attorney's legal education. At least once early in his or her career, every practicing attorney should understand how both words and actions will appear when heard "on stage," attacked by a well-prepared adversary; why it is so important always to keep at least one eye and ear on the record developing from the inception of the relationship; and what can be done to protect against the fire of battle. Even the attorney specializing exclusively in the drafting of testaments will better understand why he must include language in the instruments he drafts explaining the logic or reasoning of a testator's seemingly peculiar disposition, and why he must select testamentary witnesses who will be best able to respond properly when cross-examined regarding competence. Law today is increasingly practiced in narrow specialties, but the litigation attack is potential to all of these and must be understood and appreciated.

The Jury Voir Dire

Juries are quite uncommon in socioscientific cases, but from time to time one of the parties will insist on a right to jury trial. Many of the applicable considerations are equally pertinent to trial before a single arbiter with legal training, an individual who is, after all, subject to the same subconscious biases, prejudices, and motivations as a juror. Accordingly, some discussion of the jury process is appropriate.

The *voir dire* is the method by which a randomly determined larger panel of jurors is interrogated, so as to select the twelve or other number of petit jurors who will hear the evidence and render the verdict on the facts. The judge of course decides all questions of law. Jury selection practices vary widely around the country.

In some jurisdictions the attorneys ask the questions, in others the arbiter will inquire after considering questions the parties may submit. The common twelve-person jury has given way in some places to a smaller size; inroads have even been made on the traditional unanimous-verdict requirement. But in all jurisdictions the parties are furnished some information about each juror, such as name, address, and occupation, and there is some way in which additional information can be elicited in order to determine whether a juror should be challenged.

Challenges can be "for cause," based upon legal impediment to the juror's service (such as relationship to one of the parties), or "peremptory," the right to exclude a juror without explanation. The number of peremptories allowed also varies with the jurisdiction and the case. Although in theory the exercise of a peremptory challenge represents an absolute right that cannot be questioned, a conscious pattern of exclusion (such as challenging all persons of a particular race or religion) may have a negative impact on the remaining jurors and, where practiced by the state, may even be unlawful.

The jury selection process offers both opportunity and danger. Jurors usually correctly view themselves as important parts of the justice-dispensing system. They take their jobs very seriously and try hard to render decisions fairly and without prejudice. As a group they are generally much impressed by the trial attorney who promptly and confidently responds to the first panel of twelve potential jurors with "The jury is satisfactory," and who neither asks nor suggests any questions. In the socioscientific case, where credibility is so important, this show of confidence is most persuasive, and is a procedure worth following wherever possible.

Sometimes, however, questions must be asked. The older practice of conducting confidential personal investigations of potential jurors is coming into disfavor and may be dangerous if it suggests an attempt to influence; nor is the oft-touted juror psychological profile analysis much good. All questions must be phrased carefully so that they will not indicate to the remaining unchallenged jurors that the party is trying to obtain jurors biased in favor of its position, or that the questioner is concerned about the merits of the case. In other words, questions should communicate a sound motivation for the inquiry. In one case, for example, it was necessary to challenge, peremptorily, a musician sitting on a panel because of a substantial but unadmitted probability that he strongly favored the opposition position. Questions on *voir dire* were specifically designed to elicit information about his all-night work habits with his band. This furnished a good basis for the remaining jurors on the panel to conclude that the reason for his ultimate rejection was because the challenging party felt he would be tired and inattentive each morning in court during the long anticipated trial. This was certainly a sound motive for exercising a peremptory challenge, evidencing the challenger's confidence in his own case as well as in the justice process generally.

Each of the twelve persons on the jury "hears" the proceedings quite differently and evaluates them in a different way. Facts that evoke one kind of response in one juror may well evoke exactly the opposite in another; deciding whom to favor or what balance to maintain can pose an enigma. Each juror has a different attention span, alternating intermittently between periods of attention and periods of near daydreaming, each of varying length. It is also important to note that persuasion is enhanced when the listener, whether a legally trained arbiter or lay juror, is made to think he has discovered something for himself. Leading a single arbiter close enough to a conclusion without spilling the beans, while still being sure the conclusion is inevitable, is hard enough—doing the same with twelve persons is obviously far more difficult.

All of these problems are equally troublesome for the adversary, of course. My own experience is that the averaging of twelve different lay perceptions somehow seems to strike a balance that maximizes the chance for a fair result. Although cases do go wrong and there have been many jury miscarriages of justice which were not the fault of the parties or the arbiter, I have never personally had a twelve-person jury return a grossly inequitable verdict. I cannot say the same for nonjury trials.

Do not be afraid if faced with a jury in a socioscientific case. Do not "fold" and settle for some minimal result. The almost innumerable pluses and minuses and conflicting other considerations inevitably balance each other. One can and undoubtedly should know as much about the backgrounds of the individual jurors (and the arbiter) as is possible and proper, but it is very likely that the overall attitudes of the first twelve jurors are roughly comparable to the final carefully selected twelve. In the final analysis, emphasis upon the same trial techniques employed with the single arbiter and a straightforward approach are generally the most effective jury-trial tactics.

The Opening

The opening statement to the arbiter or jury is the party's description of what he or she expects the case to show. It is technically not argument, but anticipation and promise, telling the audience what to listen for and how each of the pieces will fit into the whole. In fact, however, it is the quintessence of argument, for it must persuade without appearing to do so.

Ordinarily the party having the burden of proof on the main issue opens first, followed immediately by the adversary, before any of the evidence is introduced. But procedures vary widely around the country and there is a growing tendency to permit a party to postpone the opening, in whole or in part, to change the order, to divide complex cases into sections with openings on each separately, or to fashion other techniques suited to a particular litigation. In the long and complex socioscientific litigation, it is wise to give advance consideration to developing and suggesting changes of this kind.

Whatever may be the case at summation time, the "fire and brimstone" type of opening is ordinarily unsuited to the socioscientific case. Credibility has rarely been established at this early a point. Moreover, the danger of a matter not turning out as one anticipates is substantial. Far better to have said nothing than to promise something which turns out to be wrong and impairs the essential consistency. I recall one criminal case in which counsel for the defendant assured the jury in his opening that his client would take the stand and testify. When the time came, however, it was clear that to testify would have been most unwise, and the defendant failed to do so. The prosecution could not have commented on a failure to testify, but in effect the defense already had. A conviction followed, certainly in part attributable to this misjudgment whatever the result might have been otherwise.

One of the rules of oral advocacy, necessarily much abused, is that an audience cannot be expected to sit and listen to a single speaker for more than 30–45 minutes, at most; within limits, the shorter the better. This rule may have to be broken during summation of a complex litigation, but a substantial effort should be made to apply it during opening. As the case unfolds, other ways can be found to explain how the evidence fits into the overall picture; only the certain should be promised in opening. If anything, underplay the strength of your case. The primary thrust should be to establish the base upon which confidence will be built during the hearing.

Demonstrative Evidence

The major, lengthy socioscientific case demands that maximum use be made of demonstrative evidence—visual aids, physical exhibits, on-site inspections, demonstrations, and anything else that can stimulate another sense and relieve tedium. Usually it makes absolutely no difference what kind of a revolver was used to commit the crime in a criminal prosecution, but the jury will still handle, examine, and pass the weapon around as though it is the most critical evidence of all. The principles of persuasion involved are even more applicable in the mundane civil, nonjury case, where glamour and excitement are minimal and the problem of boredom is serious.

The spoken word is only one method of sensory perception, and frequently not the best one at that. Quite commonly today, speakers use slide presentations to accompany their speeches, reading aloud much of what is on the slides. Many listeners sense and remember what they see on the slide far better than what they hear. When properly used, touch, taste, and smell can be even more effective.

A proper use of demonstrative evidence is essential to maintaining the attention of an arbiter, who must receive the evidence hour after hour and day after day, for weeks or even months. He or she is inevitably grateful for the relief as well as for the assistance; it reinforces credibility by showing that the party has confidence in the merits of the case and will make all efforts to explain.

Because the lawyer is usually skilled primarily in the written and spoken word, he or she should use experts in developing alternative forms of communication that make use of demonstrative evidence. (Corporate counsel frequently will have such experts available within the company.) A diagram or chart should not be just a change of the spoken word to visual form, but a communication of the concept in a new way suited to the different medium. The speaker who simply reads from slides displayed on a screen does achieve some of the objective, but only part. He or she will be far more effective if the slide shows the idea in the way the changed medium can best express it. The development of visuals to achieve this objective may be expensive and time consuming, but should be well worth doing. They should be prepared as early in the case as possible, so that they can be used on motions and in other pretrial proceedings, and the points they make become reinforced by repetition.

A good visual should be so simple an expression of the concept involved that the viewer will consider it obvious and not requiring demonstration at all. Those who specialize in this kind of work sometimes face a kind of "Catch 22" problem: Because their objective is to produce something extremely clear and simple, the purchaser may doubt its value. Clients sometimes complain of the cost when all that seemed necessary was to depict what the attorneys had suggested. In fact, however, good visuals are very much the product of communications experts, working in consultation with trial counsel. A major part of the effort is in the translation process. The forms in which the concepts are finally presented are not initially obvious at all, and are frequently arrived at only after a great deal of work and many false starts. If the basis for charges has been agreed upon in advance, this part of the cost of litigation can be one of the most cost-effective of all.

Visuals are only one kind of demonstrative evidence and, where possible, others should be designed and geared to the particular case presented. Multimedia and other new techniques are currently being explored in this rapidly developing area of artistic expertise. The presentation must be dignified and responsible, but otherwise the only limit to effectively stimulating audience perception is an arbiter's inherent conservatism. Often an actual court demonstration of a principle or test will be most useful. As always, it should be fair, even though presented from the proponent's perspective. The probably apocryphal witness who swallows the slow-acting poison and then rushes off to have his or her stomach pumped simply cannot be countenanced in rule-of-reason cases, whatever the acceptability otherwise. The risks are just too great.

Preparation for demonstrations is particularly critical. Little is as damaging as the experiment that doesn't work as described and the exhibit that fails to perform. Such inadequacies are often taken as support of the opposition case, even when they have no such significance. Always they impair credibility and cast doubt on the competence and professionalism of their proponents. There is no substitute for advance work and practice with all kinds of demonstrative evidence, sufficient to insure the result, or at least to permit satisfactory advance warning and explanation of possible failure.

Demonstrative evidence can be so compelling that adversaries will work hard to avoid it. The defendant charged with murder will try to concede that a violent death has been caused by something, so as to avoid introduction of photographs of the maimed and bloodied body; the civil litigant will concede that a product is combustible as described, rather than let the arbiter see the item go up in flames. This is called "being stipulated out of court," in that the concession eliminates much of the most telling and prejudicial evidence. Acceptance of such stipulations ordinarily should be opposed; they are not what they purport to be. They stipulate only to the fact, not to the arbiter's or jury's equally important perception of that fact.

Sometimes, of course, the real value of enhanced perception will be so obviously minimal and the proferred evidence so prejudicial that a refusal to accept an admission of the fact would be a transparent attempt to prejudice improperly, inconsistent with the rule of reason. But in most cases the right to demonstrate or show should be preserved as a means to achieve real arbiter understanding. No words describing amount of heat, length of time, size of flame, and the like can communicate the flammability of a fabric in the same fashion as the instantaneous puff of flame.

The litigant using demonstrative evidence will be on the receiving end as well, and should try to anticipate what his or her adversary will do, so as to stipulate the otherwise prejudicial evidence "out of court." Advance planning can maximize the opportunities; last-minute effort of this kind rarely is successful if adequately opposed. Early in any case an attempt should be made to admit or to stipulate anything that cannot seriously be controverted, and which might otherwise seem prejudicial. Where possible, the very first pleading can be used to avoid an issue altogether.

It should be emphasized that this technique is designed to eliminate areas that might otherwise turn out to be *unreasonably* prejudicial; it is not always unwise to permit some issues to continue on, even when one expects to lose. Arbiters and juries frequently like to compromise and grant each side something. If one insists on being right about everything, the possibility of such compromise may be lost.

Direct Witnesses

The preparation of one's own witnesses for their testimony on deposition has already been considered in Chapters 3 and 6, and many of the same principles apply equally to their testimony at trial. However, certain differences make it essential that preparation continue right on up to the time the witness completes his or her testimony at the trial. This is an area in which corporate counsel has important and sometimes primary responsibility.

The trial of a major socioscientific litigation is very much an emotional experience for all—the attorneys, the members of the litigating team, and especially the company witnesses who have been in preparation from the inception. The emotion builds as the trial approaches. There is a time and tide to their participation, which must be caught much as the crest of the last great wave the surfboarder seeks to ride in. Once missed, there is danger that all else will be anticlimax. Accordingly, the trial team must be careful not to issue false alarms about testimony and trial dates, which are rarely fixed and certain yet which the witnesses approach with great anticipation. In other respects also, corporate as well as trial counsel must take pains to understand and be sympathetic to the important emotional needs of their witnesses.

As discussed previously, a discovery deposition is generally not helpful to the individual being questioned. The witness would be better off if the deposition were not taken, for what is said can be used *against* him or her, but only rarely in his or her favor. For this reason it was suggested in Chapter 6 that answers should be as responsive, brief, and to the point as possible. Attorneys sometimes give the same advice to witnesses testifying at a hearing or trial, where the facts are finally to be decided. Usually such advice is not correct. At trial the witness is being offered *affirmatively,* for the purpose of persuading the arbiter. The adversary during cross-examination is not interested in discovery—his or her purpose is to impeach the witness's credibility, and if possible even prove him or her to be a liar. These precisely reversed objectives should be clearly explained to the witness in advance of the trial.

On direct examination, the witness should be given as much leeway and flexibility as possible, so as to be able to communicate his or her personal conviction to the arbiter. He or she should employ all the measures of persuasion discussed earlier—the affirmative approach, the effort to explain even the most complicated of concepts, the use of visuals and other demonstrative evidence. The examiner should avoid leading questions (ones to which the response can be "Yes" or "No" or some other obvious answer, or which otherwise suggest the answer). Rather, if the arbiter will permit and the witness can handle it, the witness should be given free rein and permitted to tell the whole story in answer to the fewest questions. Despite what trial lawyers may think, arbiters and juries want to hear the witnesses, not the attorneys. The less the attorney has to say while his or her own witness is testifying, the better.

It follows, of course, that the witness must be thoroughly prepared for what he or she is going to say, on direct as well as on cross-examination. Although ordinarily the witness should not read testimony, it might well have been written out earlier and rehearsed carefully, but without becoming too pat or unspontaneous. It might be added in caution that whatever the witness uses to refresh recollection, and perhaps also anything taken up to the witness stand (at deposition as well as trial) may have to be produced for the adversary's inspection. He or she should employ such aids only if both witness and counsel recognize the risks.

Preparation for cross-examination, as before, should emphasize the need for telling the truth, maintaining control of one's emotions and temper, acting respectfully, not becoming antagonistic, and the like. But the witness should also be made to understand that cross-examination is the traditional common-law method by which the law tests the validity of testimony. A good witness "grows" on cross-examination, gaining credibility and stature as given the opportunity to respond effectively to the most brutal questions. The adversary attorney is not provoking the witness because of any personal animosity, but as a way of testing whether testimony remains consistent under pressure. Witnesses rarely deliberately lie; but they all see things differently, and an understanding of the way in which they have perceived requires an understanding of their prejudices. Moreover, our senses are all different. Perhaps the witness has poor eyesight or hearing, or an inadequate sense of taste or smell. These are all things that *should* be inquired about, assuming there is an issue, in an effort to develop the truth. If the witness appreciates this, he or she will not resent the cross-examination process or lose temper.

In the absence of a specific court order to the contrary, there is usually nothing improper in speaking to one's own witness during a recess in cross-examination. But caution should be exercised in discussing the issues at the heart of the questioning. The cross-examiner on return may ask what was discussed during the break, and seek to imply that the witness was "coached" into saying something distorted or even untrue; in any event, the discussion of such issues may be made to appear as though the witness required help. To avoid this kind of suggestion, on occasion it may be wise to note on the record before the recess that one intends to confer with the witness, stating the reason.

Although the witness of course must answer directly to the cross-examiner, he or she must understand also that a witness is ultimately addressing the arbiter. A witness should not try to anticipate where the cross-examiner is going and beat him there; he or she cannot expect to defeat the experienced trial lawyer at the latter's own game. The witness should not "fence" or refuse to admit something that should be conceded, nor admit or concede what is erroneous. Sometimes questions simply cannot be answered with the "yes" or "no" on which the cross-examiner is insisting ("Have you stopped beating your wife?"), and the witness should appreciate that he or she has the right to explain in order to avoid creating the wrong impression. When confused or in need of help, the witness may properly ask the arbiter for guidance or assistance. Special caution should be exercised regarding words that have uncertain meanings, such as "long," "hard," "expensive," "beautiful," and the omnipresent socioscientific "safe" (compared to what?). He or she should be willing to admit mistake, error, and even untruth—there is no more disarming answer than "I was wrong," nor anything more calculated to pull the teeth of an expectant cross-examiner than "I lied," if these are the cases. A witness should not seek to conform to what some fellow witness may have said, or what the cross-examiner *says* was said, or what appears to be in some document, if he or she believes the contrary to be the case. The trial lawyer's use of the phrase "my witness" is in this respect a misnomer: He or she is no one's witness, but a witness for justice.

Trial counsel should be more circumspect in making objections at the trial than during deposition. The "speaking" objection, the objection designed to deflect heat from the witness, and the objection made to give the witness time to think, may well be interpreted by the arbiter as obstructing legitimate interrogation, or as evidencing concern with the merits of the issue. These practices may have been necessary at deposition, where no judge was present to rule and the interrogator was overstepping the bounds of legitimate questioning. At trial, however, such justifications are less common, for the arbiter is present to observe and decide. Moreover, objections may appear to arbiters and jurors as inherently obstructive, and they should be employed only to serve a valid purpose.

The above is not to suggest, however, that objections should only be made when the objectionable matter is considered seriously prejudicial. To follow such a practice during a lengthy trial would very soon pinpoint the litigant's sources of concern. Sometimes, indeed, objections should be made regarding relatively minor matters in preparation for contesting some serious issue and to obscure the greater concern.

Trial counsel in rule-of-reason litigations should also be careful about using the other common timing devices so often employed to protect a witness or to gain an edge during cross-examination. If the court regularly adjourns at 4:30 PM, timing one's own witness to complete his or her direct examination at 4 PM *can* effectively cut short the cross; stretching out the cross-examination of an opposition witness so as to have overnight or a weekend to study the transcript *can* be helpful; shifting the logical order in which witnesses are adduced *can* achieve a similar result. But these techniques (similar to the deliberate last-minute service of legal papers at the close of business on a Friday or just before a holiday, thereby cutting short the adversary's time to respond), can also backfire if used too often or too obviously. The result may be to lose the advantage sought (by having the witness held over or cut short), to impair the examination, *and* to persuade the arbiter that the asserted rule of reason is itself a tactic and fiction. There is a fine dividing line between devices of this kind and the "tricks" prohibited by the rule of reason. They should be approached with caution.

Expert Witnesses

One kind of direct witness is of particular importance to the socio-scientific litigation: the expert scientific or technical witness. The key issues in such cases usually turn on matters that require some special training or background, which the layperson does not possess. The expert is entitled to state opinion; the layperson is not.

Although most persons think of witnesses with advanced graduate degrees as the only individuals qualified to be court "experts," the only requirement in fact is that the witness be shown to have some knowledge which renders his or her opinion worthy of special consideration. A businessperson with thirty years of marketing experience in a certain area may well be qualified as an expert in that market, even though he or she was a high-school "drop-out." An assembly-line worker who has drilled holes in metal brackets for a lifetime may be an expert on the time required to drill such holes. Once the qualifications have been found to be sufficient, the witness may testify to his or her opinion within that area of expertise, without much limit. What is said and how it is said do not affect the admissibility of the testimony any more than with the fact witness, but only the weight that should be given to it.

The inclination to testify to matters beyond the witness's area of special competence is one of the major pitfalls for the expert scientific or technical witness. The assembly-line worker who has qualified as an expert to testify regarding drilling is unlikely to consider himself qualified to discuss brain surgery; but for some reason the expert with several graduate degrees will stray almost deliberately. The Nobel prize winner in physics will expound regarding genetics; the biochemist regarding statistics; the mathematician regarding astronomy. If these highly qualified persons can be limited to their fields, the lay cross-examiner is hard put to touch them. When they go afar, they become grist for his mill.

Although some jurisdictions now permit increased discovery from experts, the practice is still rare and they usually will testify at trial without prior exposure to the pretrial deposition. Special emphasis on limiting them to what they can competently say is therefore of particular importance.

Some attorneys will go to great lengths to retain so-called "independent" experts to testify at a hearing or trial. Experts are expensive in most cases and the need to pay an outsider and to train someone new can increase costs substantially. It is difficult to see why anyone considers an expert who is paid a large fee any more "independent" than a person with equal qualifications from the corporation's own laboratories, who has been saying the same thing from the inception even before the specific dispute arose. My experience is that arbiters often view "independent" experts with some doubt, because they pretend to be something they are not (i.e., "independent"). In addition, arbiters have viewed so many "battles of experts" in which people of the same high qualifications state opposite conclusions that they view all with suspicion.

The independent expert who is *really* uncompensated directly or indirectly is something else again, but (assuming he or she is not an extremist) such a person is hard to come by and ordinarily cannot be expected to devote the substantial time required to be a part of the litigation team. Accordingly, even if there are such volunteers available, whenever possible the company should also use experts from its own staff as witnesses at the hearing. Their testimony is no more colored by their employment than that of any other employee. And of course the saving in expense, and benefits to internal company education, can be substantial.

Cross-Examination

Much of what is ordinarily treated under the heading "cross-examination" has necessarily already been treated elsewhere—the need to prepare carefully and intensively so as to have maximum opportunity to think; the importance of fact controls; the requirement that witnesses be treated with courtesy and respect until the right to attack aggressively has been demonstrated on the evidence to the arbiter; the extraordinary dangers of inquiring into collateral matters, such as the fee the witness is receiving or his or her personal habits and motivations; the need to ask simple, short, "tight" questions that the witness cannot evade; the significance of a scientist's demonstration of bias and hostility, and the attack on his or her testimony outside the acknowledged area of expertise. All the cautions suggested in connection with preparation of one's own witnesses and case generally have their counterparts here. But again certain additional considerations deserve emphasis in the rule-of-reason case.

The trial attorney obviously is at a great advantage in any exchange with a witness. Cross-examination is the attorney's field of expertise, and he or she knows its rules as intimately as the witness knows his or her business. Moreover, the attorney is right at home and the witness in strange territory. There is an understandable tendency for the attorney to play with words and be "cute," even if not rude and unpleasant. This kind of conduct is never acceptable. In the rule-of-reason case it is even worse, because the attorney is the main spokesperson for the corporate client and the conduct will be considered as evidencing the company's disdain and disrespect for the individual. Corporate counsel should urge the trial attorney to treat each opposition witness as though the witness were a corporate employee, and only go on the offensive in these regards if clearly justified by the nature of the witness's conduct. Whenever possible, the witness should be given an escape or way out of a trap, so that he or she need not be unnecessarily embarrassed. It is rarely possible to convince someone that he or she has acted badly or is wrong, and the person who goes away aggrieved may find a chance to retaliate. Neither single arbiter nor juror likes to see the defeated made to suffer; sympathy is with the underdog. This is not to suggest that the witness who lies should not be exposed; but in most cases allowing a witness to retreat and lick his or her wounds will be a charitable gesture appreciated by all and in the corporation's overall interest.

There is an old trial-law rule that a cross-examiner should never ask a question unless he or she knows the answer. Obviously this has its exceptions. When *in extremis,* for example, where defeat seems certain, what harm can exploratory questions do? But the rule has special validity in the socioscientific case. Proper pretrial preparation should have eliminated most areas of uncertainty. And the risks of a damaging answer harming credibility are usually much too great to justify any relatively minor point that might be made.

The opposition expert who refuses to answer a question directly and throws up new smokescreens by the use of technical language is a common hostile witness. Sometimes the best way to deal with such a witness is to ask the arbiter to direct that he or she answer the question. But frequently the better tactic is to keep asking the identical question over and over, thereby repeatedly underscoring the witness's hostility. Repeating the same question, "Was the cage door open?" twenty-five times, each time with a different answer about following ordinary procedures, lack of significance of another animal getting into the cage, availability of water from other sources, and the like, can be most telling. The final angry, exhausted "yes" becomes a trial climax. As in so many other areas, dogged persistence can be the key to success.

Cross-examination in the socioscientific case, with numerous expert and lay witnesses, also may call for some modification of normal impeachment technique. The trial attorney must of course have some knowledge of the expert witness's specialty, but is usually no real match for the expert in this area. Even when the attorney has a friendly expert to help (as he or she always should when possible), in the heat of cross-examination the lawyer is very much alone. Cross-examination under these circumstances (and indeed quite generally) is commonly designed to develop the few relatively minor errors or mistakes found in the witness's testimony on direct, with the hope of persuading the arbiter or jury that these errors are symptomatic of the whole. If, however, a small number of errors in the expert's testimony is revealed and a large number of errors with the lay witnesses who follow, the arbiter may mistakenly conclude that the expert's testimony is more accurate than the layperson's. It may accordingly be well to hold back on cross-examination with some witnesses, even if minor errors can be developed, in order to strike more effectively at a key expert. One cannot hope to destroy all adverse witnesses, and there is usually no reason to try.

Finally, it bears repetition that witnesses can grow on cross-examination. Better to state a quick "no questions" when a witness concludes, if there is nothing to impeach or only minor damage has been inflicted, than to offer a witness the opportunity to become more convincing. Often the best cross-examination is no cross-examination at all.

Burden of Proof

"Burden of proof" is a strictly legal phrase, much used—and abused—in socioscientific cases. It is important in initial licensing and registration contexts, but has relatively little real significance in ultimate determination of the risk/benefit environmental disputes in which it so commonly appears.

The phrase can have two meanings: The first and most common meaning is that one party to the proceeding bears the risk of nonpersuasion—that party must satisfy the arbiter of the issues by some level or quantum of evidence, or lose. The second meaning relates as well to the level of evidence required of the plaintiff in the common civil case, which is a simple "preponderance," or 50+ percent.

There are of course other levels (or "burdens") of evidence which may be required in other situations. Thus, in the usual criminal case, the amount by which the sovereign must prove its case is a level "beyond a reasonable doubt"; in administrative or appellate proceedings, amounts of proof required are expressed in terms such as "clear and convincing evidence," "substantial evidence," and "clearly erroneous."

The question of who bears the "burden of proof" in either of these senses is significant only in a very close case. Such cases do occur, of course, but it is uncommon for the evidence to be so finely balanced that one party or the other is successful on the ground of burden alone. In socioscientific environmental litigations, where the term "burden of proof" has been so much debated, the arguments really turn on the level of evidence which should be required and on another completely separate litigation concept, the "burden of coming forward with proof." Yet because of the confusion regarding terminology, industry is sometimes made to appear as though it favors a risk course of action unless someone else demonstrates a 50+ percent preponderance of persons benefited. This is ridiculous, but has still seriously damaged industry credibility in these matters.

"Burden of coming forward" with evidence or proof, also termed the "burden of proceeding," means that a matter will not be questioned until some legitimate area of concern has been established. One doesn't initiate a long-term, vastly expensive inquiry into the ozone layer, for example, unless there is *some* significant reason to believe that the product being questioned may be endangering the atmosphere, with anticipated adverse consequences to the environment. The "level" or "amount" of evidence required here is certainly far less than in the ultimate risk/benefit analysis, and therefore even further removed from the preponderance-of-the-evidence concept.

There is another burden concept of relatively minor importance in this context, the burden of presenting a *prima facie* case. This simply means that the party having such a burden must adduce sufficient evidence to warrant a verdict in its favor, employing the appropriate test as to the level of evidence required, if the other party fails to present *any* evidence.

There is no present way of quantifying the almost infinite considerations involved in environmental risk/benefit analysis, but a hypothetical example will be useful in clarifying these concepts. Assume the benefits of vaccinating against smallpox in the United States are deemed sufficient to justify the serious illness of one in every ten million persons to whom the vaccine is administered.

In a litigation evaluating the acceptability of continued vaccination in this country, the issue would then be whether the risks of illness are any greater than 1:10,000,000. If not, the product continues in use; if so, the product is banned. If the evidence is in such equal balance that the arbiter simply cannot decide either way, the "burden of proof" concept comes into play and the party on the attack (a lay expression, necessary to avoid the myriad considerations involved in deciding who in fact has the burden of proof) loses. But in view of the obvious uncertainties in this kind of case, it is rare indeed that the evidence will be so finely balanced.

Assume that after the product has received approval in such a contest a charge is made that there is also a danger of death from liver cancer, striking one in every five million persons receiving the vaccine, but only twenty-five or more years after its administration. The party making such a charge has the obligation of presenting *some* evidence to justify reopening the inquiry; a simple cry of danger, unaccompanied by any foundation, should obviously not suffice. Whether or not the party making the charge will have the burden of proof in the litigation contest itself, it has the "burden of coming forward" with sufficient evidence to warrant a new inquiry.

The term "burden of proof" is often inaccurately used by both industry and its opposition when what is really involved is a debate over the "amount" of proof that should be required, or the "burden of coming forward" concept. Yet because the term has an apparent lay meaning, as stated above industry is sometimes made to sound as though it believes a course of action is justified unless its opponents can, for example, show that the number of anticipated deaths will exceed the number of anticipated lives saved. Extreme as this may be, it is the public perception which counts, and much credibility has been lost as a result.

Those who seek to deal with the important socioscientific issues in a rational manner must assume the obligation of employing language that is clear to the public making the final decisions. Trial counsel, moving from case to case, cannot be expected to understand the public-interest considerations involved and corporate counsel consequently must assume this important responsibility. He or she should not only see that trial counsel understands, but take whatever opportunity is presented to write, speak, and otherwise publicly explain the issues involved.

Evidence

The rules of evidence, and especially their application, vary widely from jurisdiction to jurisdiction, tribunal to tribunal, and even from arbiter to arbiter. Some administrative-law judges in agency proceedings, where the strict rules of evidence have never been applicable, are far more rigorous in their applications of the older technical hearsay rules, for example, than even judges in those state courts that have not adopted the more liberal modern concepts. Appeals concerning rulings on evidence are rarely successful, so that knowledge of the local practice and the proclivities of the arbiter concerned are essential. Adherence to the requirements is, of course, the trial lawyer's province, but corporate counsel can be particularly helpful in those agencies and tribunals in which he or she has had experience, and before which the trial attorney may not have practiced.

After more than a decade of effort, and a much longer period during which the need was recognized, statutory federal rules of evidence became effective July 1, 1975. These replaced the confusion of existing civil procedure, which applied state evidence law when no federal practice controlled, and of federally developed criminal procedure.

The new federal evidence rules are short and should be reviewed by corporate counsel managing any litigation. Even though they are applicable only in the federal courts, other tribunals frequently follow the spirit and sometimes even the letter of the generally more well-considered and modern federal approach. Moreover, oldtimers at the bar often continue with their former ways by virtue of a kind of implicit "grandfather clause" in new procedural rules, courteously accorded them by judges and colleagues at the bar. In this case corporate counsel may even gain a jump on trial counsel, because the rules are so new and unconstrued and he or she has less to unlearn.

Two of the new rules are of particular significance to socio-scientific cases. Rule 501 provides (in part) that privilege "shall be governed by the principles of the common law as they may be interpreted by the courts of the United States in the light of reason and experience." This pretty much leaves the law of privilege in its present state, ending much effort within the United States Supreme Court and elsewhere to limit and restrict privilege. The result may well be a legal atmosphere more conducive to the assertion of privilege in future cases.

Rule 804 (b) (5) provides for an exception to the hearsay rule where, among other things, "the general purposes of these rules and the interests of justice will best be served by admission of the statement into evidence." It remains to be seen how this provision will be applied, but on its face it suggests considerable loosening of the rules. Almost anything but the "kitchen sink" seems to be received in evidence "for what it is worth," when offered by government or consumer groups *against* corporate defendants in socioscientific cases. This rule indicates that corporate parties may now be able to achieve the same benefits. Adherence to the specific advance-notice requirements of Rule 804 (b) (5) is of course essential.

The Court Reporter

The stenographic reporter who records and transcribes the proceedings is all too frequently taken for granted and his or her importance overlooked in socioscientific litigations. This is unwise. The final, transcribed record in socioscientific cases is ordinarily far more significant than in private disputes. Many administrative proceedings are conducted by arbiters whose only function is to see that the record is correct; they do not even recommend a decision. Instead the decision is rendered by the head of the agency or department on the basis of the record alone or as it may be supplemented by other advice received. Appeals, also necessarily limited to the record, are also more common in socioscientific cases, where the issues can be of far-reaching importance to society generally. In addition, the kinds of problems involved have a way of going on and on, so that the record in one proceeding is useful in another at a distant time and place as evidence of what was done, for cross-examination purposes or otherwise.

Court stenographers and transcribers are just as human as the rest of us, so that some error will inevitably appear in any work they do. In the socioscientific case, replete with technicality and esoteric science, and taking place over long periods of time under great pressure, there is much danger of compounding this error. Transcripts are often purchased on a "daily" basis, to be completed the night of the hearing for review in advance of the next day's proceedings. Stenographers must spell each other every half hour or so. Their notes must be read by a number of different typists, often hired on an *ad hoc* basis and relatively inexperienced. Modern recording and electronic data-processing techniques may one day change all this, but for the present the litigant must personally take steps to help insure accuracy.

In any socioscientific case worth its salt, the court stenographer should be furnished a glossary of terms and names, containing every special word expected to be used in the proceeding. When an important statement or admission is given, the reporter should be asked to read it back. (Sometimes this technique is also a good litigation tactic to emphasize an admission that has been given or some other important development, or to give a witness time to think, but it should be employed carefully and not to excess.) If the record cannot be reviewed immediately, counsel should write down the statement and ask the reporter to mark his or her notes for checking at the next break. Trial counsel will usually read the transcript in preparation for the next day's session, and should mark any errors noted. In addition, a paralegal should be assigned to review in depth each transcript each night (assuming the case runs on from day to day), and prepare a list of corrections promptly. Sometimes the court reporter will even furnish a transcript in draft and agree to compare the suggestions against his or her notes, accepting the corrections where appropriate before distributing the final copies. This is uncommon, however, because the pressures of time are so great and the list of corrections is normally simply submitted to the tribunal the following morning. Usually a stipulation of acceptance can be arranged; the opposition will often agree to the proposed corrections without even reading them. Where there is any dispute, however, the witness can verify the change if he or she is still testifying, or proposing counsel can express his or her recollection and let the arbiter decide which version is correct.

It is not always necessary to go to such lengths to insure maximum accuracy of a transcript. Sometimes it will be clear that the arbiter's determination will be final, with no chance for appeal or other future use of the transcript. But more commonly the significant effort justified is not undertaken simply because there are so many other things to do and the matter has been overlooked. Even the chief executive of the corporate party will be permitted to testify regarding important company policy, without any effort to verify accuracy of the transcript until the proceeding is concluded. There is no excuse for this; the expense is minimal by comparison with the total. Corporate counsel should insist that it be done, where possible assuming responsibility for supplying the needed paralegal assistance.

The Summation

If the opening is the "quintessence" of argument, because it must persuade without appearing to do so, the summation is the ultimate of advocacy. The trial lawyer must bring together all that has been accomplished during what may have been a lengthy proceeding, marshal his or her arguments, answer the assertions of the adversary, anticipate the unasked questions of the arbiter, consider all from the vantage points of others (this, of course, is partly speculation), and do all this with at most a few hours or overnight for final preparation. Summation calls for every talent the trial lawyer has to offer, and he or she knows the resulting performance will be watched and graded. The pressures are enormous. Whatever may have been their earlier relationship, at this point corporate counsel's responsibility is to provide the trial lawyer support and nothing more. He or she should not question or "bug" and should ensure that the demands of others on the trial attorney's attention are kept to the absolute minimum. Although corporate counsel should furnish whatever help is sought in the final preparation, he or she must be sensitive to the important ego considerations involved and criticize only constructively and with compliment.

Even here, however, corporate counsel can be of assistance to trial counsel in the socioscientific litigation, by advising him or her well in advance of two especially significant concerns, one positive and one negative. On the positive side, it is important for the corporate party to sum up in as objective a manner as possible, citing the maximum of quotations and citations from the transcripts of witnesses' testimony and exhibits. Some appeal to public-policy considerations and emotion is appropriate, of course, but this should be supported by what the witnesses have said and written. This citation approach is necessary even if it means a longer summation, violating the principle of brevity. The reason, of course, is corporate credibility. One day perhaps the assertions of corporate trial counsel in socioscientific cases may be received on the same basis as those of government and "public interest" groups, but this is not the case today. Appeals to emotion and prejudice are best matched by reference to chapter and verse and fine logic.

On the negative side, trial counsel should be advised that the adversary summation may well take just the opposite tack, concentrating on broad charges and claims, and filling in with specific references to the evidence only as alleged "examples." Frequently this will be justified as necessary in order to compress the summation into the short time stated to be available, which may well be a self-imposed deadline. This is the technique of summation in the criminal conspiracy case, the "darling of the prosecutors": The brief summation painting the outline of the conspiracy and furnishing one or two details of each part as "examples" obscures the fact that there are not sufficient other "examples" to prove all the necessary elements of the charge beyond a reasonable doubt.

The answer to this technique is to insist that the opposition be given as much time as it needs to complete its summation, and try to block any effort at proof by isolated "example." If the practice persists, each charge and example must be analyzed in light of the record. Where there is no jury, written summaries can be handed up for inspection by the arbiter at his or her later convenience. Sometimes the arbiter can be persuaded to accept briefs on the subjects, which of course can point up the defects more effectively.

Exciting as the summation may be, it is becoming less and less important in socioscientific cases. The summation reaches its peak of importance in jury trials, and only rarely are juries used. In the more common administrative tribunal and single-judge proceeding, the corporate litigant should seek in effect to sum up as the case unfolds, beginning with a prehearing memorandum outlining what the evidence is expected to show, and following with memoranda of fact summarizing segments of the litigation as the witnesses testify and the evidence is received. These memos should be submitted even if the opposition refuses to do the same; indeed, submission by one side gives it an advantage, even though copies must be furnished to the adversary (along with any other materials submitted to the arbiter—any attempt at *ex parte* communication with an arbiter is most dangerous and unwise as well as usually improper).

Towards the end of nonjury administrative and judicial proceedings, arbiters today commonly require the submission of proposed written findings of fact (and conclusions of law), and thereafter posthearing memoranda of various kinds. But advocacy need not decline as a result; it should instead mature and develop techniques far more suited to the complexity and importance of these kinds of litigations. Summation is an art, not a time frame or an approach to any single sense. The art of advocacy thrives equally well in the written as in the oral environment.

Postverdict Action

Few moments are as emotionally tense or as thrilling as that magnificent few-second lifetime before the foreperson answers the judge's question, "What is the verdict?" The trial lawyer's heart seems almost to stop; sometimes one hardly hears the response. The excitement is not the same when the judge or administrative tribunal announces a decision, usually long after the trial, but it is still enormous. The product of thousands of hours of work and all one's talents and resources is finally to be judged and evaluated, with major consequences to career, reputation, and client.

It is understandable that there is an almost equally striking posttrial letdown. The trial attorneys typically take at least a few days vacation—more if possible. Witnesses and executives turn to other matters temporarily postponed, sometimes specifically to the day following trial. Only a minimum staff remains on hand to handle the "clean-up" work of packing documents, returning files, paying bills, and the like. And this staff is ordinarily the least experienced and qualified to handle important strategy questions.

Yet the period immediately following a decision is in fact the time calling for the greatest ingenuity and imagination in fashioning a revised strategy to handle the problem at issue. The other side is equally stunned and off-guard. Minor concessions following a victory may avoid a lengthy, expensive, and uncertain appeal; a new approach following defeat may make possible a settlement that will achieve at least some part of the underlying objective.

More commonly the result of the trial is neither victory nor defeat, but some combination of the two, calling for reevaluations, modifications of earlier anticipations, and new authorizations. The party that studies the matter first may be able to take action which concludes some issues, or which results in public acceptance of the outcome. This is not the time to vacation, but to study, confer, and analyze even harder and more intensively—just as soon as those involved can think clearly. (*Always* try to avoid acting when under any kind of pressure and tension. If action is mandatory, at least seek to consult others who are detached and able to reflect calmly.) The rewards of postponing well-earned relief to a later time will be substantial.

Appeals

Corporate counsel with little actual courtroom experience may understandably be reluctant to manage the work of his or her trial attorney too closely—the trial lawyer is the expert, and his or her artistic effort may suffer if too many constraints are imposed. Corporate counsel seem to feel the same regarding appellate work, but here there is no such justification. The techniques of advocacy involved are very much the same as those corporate counsel employs in his or her everyday work of written and oral persuasion; there is ordinarily much more time to study and consider.

Even if staffing and other concerns make it unwise to handle the major part of appellate practice in-house, corporate counsel should participate intimately in the appellate process, in at least as careful a fashion as suggested earlier in connection with pretrial preparation. He or she should consider proposed approaches to brief writing before the drafting begins and should review the early drafts as they are prepared. Corporate staff experts should themselves prepare those sections dealing with aspects of the law or facts in which they are expert; they might also participate in oral argument of these areas if the tribunal will permit such sharing. Paralegals who worked on the trial can marshal the trial transcript and exhibits, and prepare what may be a most voluminous record on appeal. If electronic data-processing techniques were employed earlier, it may even be possible to print, offset, or otherwise duplicate in-house the record and major portions of the briefs at low cost. Tribunals are becoming sensitive to high litigation costs and have relaxed considerably the earlier rule requiring typesetting and printing. Many will permit any form of appellate submission which appears neat and clean and is easy to handle.

There are as many different techniques of writing a brief as there are of trying a case, and most can be equally successful or unsuccessful, depending on the quality of the final product. But once again certain considerations are particularly applicable to the lengthy, complex, socioscientific case.

An effort should be made at the very outset of the first brief to distill, sympathetically but fairly, a single, simple, key point that can be quickly and easily grasped: "The heart of this case is whether animal experimentation will be permitted, to alleviate human suffering"; or "This appeal will decide whether industry may continue to exercise riparian rights in a river, where the industrial production essential to community well-being in no way impairs the quality of that river." Judges and senior administrators have little time to read and absorb the scientific details of a lengthy litigation. It is naive as well as foolhardy to assume that they can understand even a minor fraction of what the parties have developed and presented over so long a period, or what the arbiter below decided after weeks or months of receiving evidence. They necessarily rely heavily on their clerks and assistants. Their first impression may well determine their final reaction as well, and the instructions they give as to what the decision will be. That first impression should be focused on the major public-policy issue, ordinarily their real interest, in such a way that the affirmative benefits of the desired course are emphasized.

The other important points of argument and contention should not be omitted, of course. They should be organized into points and subpoints, with emphasis on the title and the very first sentence in each. Watching oral arguments, one will see that judges and administrative officials often "skim read" briefs, looking just at the headings and what follows immediately thereafter. This is not always the case; some appellate tribunals come to the oral arguments well prepared, having read and digested much of the briefs. But with so many cases to handle, and no access to experts who can patiently explain what is involved to the trial and corporate attorney, even here understanding is superficial and limited. Clerks and assistants do much more, but any attorney who has worked his or her way through a many-thousand-page appellate record, reviewing exhibit references back and forth, and without any knowledge of how things sounded or what they looked like, knows how much the most intensively prepared appellate perception differs from the reality of what went on below.

Emphasis on first sentences and point hearings should not result in omission of any of the arguments. There is no way of being certain as to what will ultimately be persuasive. An opinion usually has to be written, and its preparation may be expedited or its strength enhanced because of something not initially considered important. But the danger of losing the significant in the mass of detail should not be overlooked. Matters of minor value should be placed in footnotes or appendices; pains should be taken to be certain that they too are expressed in as simple and clear a fashion as possible. Emphasis should be placed on what is important by underscoring, italics, boldface, use of other different types, color, indentation and spacing, reproduction of exhibits, and the like. The visual sense may be the only perception involved in brief writing, but there are many different ways of stimulating even a single sense, and they should all be employed as appropriate. Needless to say, the specific tribunal rules must be followed and gimmicks and injudicious techniques should be avoided. But usually permission can be obtained to bend even the strictest rules for good cause, and the motion requesting the tribunal for permission to do so may itself have value in the persuasion process.

Without being too obvious about it, pains should also be taken to draft the brief so that appropriate portions can be lifted out with minor language changes and included in the tribunal's opinion. What better way to insure that any further appeal will be on the best possible terms? What easier way also to persuade subconsciously the busy, overworked appellate judges to decide in one's favor?

Here as elsewhere in litigation, weak points should be dealt with, not ignored in the hope that the adversary will forget them. To do otherwise impairs credibility and loses the important initial opportunity to present any weaknesses in the most favorable light.

Oral argument of the appeal offers an opportunity to stimulate perception through another sense, and should rarely if ever be waived. It may be the only chance to have a real and personal impact on those who will decide the case. Reading of the brief at any length is inexcusable—an abdication of the opportunity to persuade. Even tribunals accustomed to extending every courtesy to members of the bar will frequently not permit it. Reading of an argument directed to the hearing sense may be acceptable if necessary, although it is certainly not desirable. But when done, the reader must be ready to stop, change direction, answer questions, and react whenever and however his or her perception of the listener suggests. Here, as elsewhere, good oral advocacy calls for carefully preparing the argument in detail, in writing if possible, knowing it by heart, and then delivering it "extemporaneously."

First-rate litigation "spontaneity" is in fact the result of intense preparation.

Conceptually, appellate tribunals decide only the law and consider themselves bound by what the arbiter found to be the facts in the lower tribunal, unless his or her decision was "clearly erroneous" or not supported by "substantial evidence," or wrong in some other major respect. But in fact the persons who sit on appellate bodies are also just as human as the rest of us, and just as influenced by their own feelings and attitudes and backgrounds. In some cases their decisions may be so positively determined by the law that there is no escape. But usually there is enough flexibility to permit the decision to be what they want it to be. The techniques and approaches may be different, but the need to persuade is every bit as vital as in the earlier hearing. To the extent proper and possible, the most favorable appellate tribunal should be searched for and applied to; the most favorable members selected; and the backgrounds, proclivities, and earlier decisions of those on the panel investigated.

Frequently in the socioscientific case, it will be necessary to request some kind of interim relief while the appeal is pending. Stays of lower tribunal determinations are quite commonly granted if serious prejudice would otherwise result and the delay in enforcing the decision is not likely to cause great harm. Appellate counsel should use the opportunity afforded in connection with the application for a stay to begin the process of persuasion. Although the chances for different final arbiters are usually more substantial, appellate tribunals are no more able than lower tribunal arbiters to isolate the beginnings and ends of the persuasion process into neat little packages of "appeal" or "trial."

Most jurisdictions today have rules that seek to limit interim or interlocutory appeals taken before the lower tribunal proceeding has come to its final conclusion. Despite this, there is usually some way in which an important preliminary lower tribunal ruling can be reviewed by a higher tribunal, either through the appellate process of reviewing "extraordinary" kinds of matters, through separate writs such as mandamus, or otherwise. Trial lawyers not accustomed to socioscientific cases or not trained in the appellate process should be encouraged to search for some such procedure when it appears necessary.

When all is said and done, however, only a relatively small number of major socioscientific cases are reversed on appeal. Reversals make headlines; affirmances and the much greater number of cases in which appeals are not taken, do not. It is the hearing or trial that counts most, and on which the greatest emphasis must be placed. The "we'll take an immediate appeal" approach rarely works.

The Challenge to Corporate Counsel

Chapter **8**

Corporate counsel today have an exciting and perhaps unique opportunity to do what lawyers have done so often throughout our common-law history: help lead the way into a new and better society. They must do this not only because it is good and right that they do so, but because it is in the best interests of their corporate clients, which they are required to represent as they best can.

The bar at large has thus far failed to furnish evidence that it will be able soon to improve ethics and quality of practice. Despite Watergate and the burgeoning protests regarding the trial bar, little of immediate effect has been accomplished and little appears on the horizon. The vacuum is waiting to be filled.

Whatever its earlier problems, much of modern corporate general management is beginning to appreciate the demands—and the opportunities—of the new society. Long-range social, environmental, and economic considerations are more and more a major part of corporate decision making. Corporations are not just asserting property and other traditional common-law rights in reaction to developments, but are beginning to play a vital affirmative role in shaping the new society. It may yet develop that they will be key intermediates between the much desired individualistic determination of a past era, no longer possible in a complex, over-populated world, and the totalitarian central control we resolutely oppose. The process, however, is just beginning. It needs all the help it can get, especially on the major legal battlegrounds where corporate presence is on the public firing line and where credibility has so often suffered.

Corporate counsel can help furnish the needed assistance, achieve major cost savings, and provide vital new leadership to the legal profession as well, by adopting the rule of reason to govern their clients' internal conduct and by insisting that the same rule be applied by all outside counsel. Gradually the good will shut out the bad; as the practice becomes general, it will become compulsory to trial counsel as well. Those who continue to practice the sporting and game approaches will discover through repeated defeat and loss that there is a better way, and that it is a happier way.

But leadership demands that there be maximum effort to achieve the goal. Throughout history lawyers have led by teaching, speaking, writing, and marshaling their resources. Corporate counsel advocating the rule of reason should do the same. The law schools need their help in practice and ethics training; the law journals and the media and public generally will welcome their explanations and advice. They should join each other in a "corporate counsel bar association" to advance the rule of reason, in the same fashion that other legal specialists have joined into trial lawyers' and international lawyers' bar associations. Working singly and together they can have great influence and power, sharing experiences and information, policing improper practices, and taking whatever other action is proper and possible to benefit their clients, their profession, and society at large. They can measure their success by the speed with which the words "integrity," "morality," "honesty," "ethics," and "truth" can be used without qualification to describe our system of justice.

The time is right. The opportunity is great. The risks are minimal. The rewards are enormous. The legal profession and society await only the call to arms.